The Last Election

The Last Election

An American Prophecy

James Glenn Reynolds

Library of Congress Control Number:		2014909649
ISBN:	Hardcover	978-1-4990-2640-5
	Softcover	978-1-4990-2641-2
	eBook	978-1-4990-2639-9

This book was printed in the United States of America.

Rev. date: 06/04/2014

To order additional copies of this book, contact:
Xlibris LLC
1-888-795-4274
www.Xlibris.com
Orders@Xlibris.com
619163

Contents

For my sons, their children, and grandchildren
that they may always know
God and human freedom
in America.

Preface

I first became alarmed over the direction of our country during the stagflation days of the 1970s following our defeat in Vietnam, the Nixon behavior, and the growth in federal regulatory activity ensuing from the Great Society legislation. I was a younger man then and took time out to tilt at political windmills, standing for federal office in 1978. Having exhausted my savings in this endeavor, and with a family to support, I returned to earning a livelihood.

It was not until after the 2012 election, in my seventieth year, that I set out to write this book. Yet throughout these past three-plus decades, as I, along with most Americans, have been witnessing the ebbing of our great nation, I have continually harkened back to a book I read in 1981 when it was first published.

At the time, I was acquainted with an editor at Houghton Mifflin who alerted me to this wildly diverse and jumbled account of a wandering reporter that he was valiantly trying to meld into some sort of book that could be held together. The result was *Nine Nations of North America*, a terrific effort by author Joel Garreau, his editor, and the staff that assisted them in it all. Garreau found our many souls and brought them fully to life for us to consider, respect, and honor. He was really on to something, and I knew it then. I just didn't fully understand all the implications.

The urgency of my work here is driven partly by my advancing age and also by the recent work of two historians: Niall Ferguson's *Civilization* (2011) and Fergus Bordewich's *America's Great Debate* (2012). Each of these books, one an analysis of the unique attributes of the West as civilization and the other an analysis of the earnest debates of 1850, bear tangentially on the subject matter of my effort here in that they served as inspiration for me to "just do it" and gave me very useful points of reference.

It is my firm conviction that we are once again heading for a Last Election here in the United States. In 1860, we had a Last Election. Today many of the same societal conditions are present, while other aspects of our society are strikingly different. In 1860, we had survived fifty plus years of discomfort between the northern and southern societies over the institution of slavery plus ten years from 1850 in futile debate over several aspects of the issue. Today we have survived forty years of discomfort between largely urban and largely rural societies over the enormous and incessant growth of a Central Authority in Washington, DC, plus nearly five years since 2008 in futile debate over several aspects of the issue. Our ability to govern a nation of fifty states is as hopelessly broken as was our ability to govern a nation of thirty-two states in 1860.

The most significant similarity between these two eras is that the sides in the debate define themselves as states and governments in states. The North and the South were defined and represented by state governments in those regions. Four border slave states did not secede. Today we have the red states and the blue states. And in the blue border states, we have generally southern regions of these states that are solidly red. Regional division with governmental units in these regions in tune with the regional mood creates the pathway to a Last Election.

The differences between the two times are as significant as they are interesting. In 1850, we were beginning to feel a "manifest destiny" borne of the Mexican War victory, annexation of the territory that would become Utah, Nevada, Arizona, New Mexico, and part of Texas which had joined the Union as had California. We now had a continent to settle and exploit. But we couldn't get along on the matter of slavery. And if we were to settle the continent and admit territories as states, the matter of slavery had to be dealt with. We had no good choices because we were hopelessly divided on the issue. The democratic process could bring a marginal victory to one side or the other, but not with the consent of the loser. The Last Election was in 1860. Then we broke up. Then we had war.

Today our principal problem is debt. We are going broke and will have to renege on trillions of dollars of promises. We have lost our empire and have no energy to engage in empire building. We don't have a national mission driving us.

We are adrift, and yet our national Central Authority keeps growing every year, gathering into its control more and more of every American's daily life. And we cannot get along on the issue of ever increasing central authority capturing us all back into human bondage.

People in the blue states largely accept a Way of Life that is provided for and directed by a central government authority. People in the red states largely favor a Way of Life that maximizes individual human freedom and relegates the role of government to that of protector and facilitator, but not the provider. Marginal victories and defeats in democratic elections do not result in either broad consensus or consent by the loser. Elections are now brutal contests in a war of destruction. No one seeks consensus, only victory and destruction of the loser. We are hopelessly divided on our Way of Life. Yet we must deal with our looming debt disaster. We have no good choices.

In these social environments another element is present. Let's call it the 10 percent factor. When people are content or working hard or basically unafraid, no small minority can rile them up for chaos. But when people are afraid, out of work, or unhappy about their future, the 10 percent become very powerful. In the 1850s, the abolitionists were a small minority in the North, but they were able to play their game on the unhappiness of their fellow citizens with capture of runaway slaves in their communities. In the South, the radical slave owners were able to play their game on the general fear that their Way of Life was in jeopardy. Lincoln gets elected with 39 percent of the vote. Not exactly a mandate. Then someone does something dumb. And the 10 percent on either side have their day. The other 80 percent who just want to work and raise a family in peace with their community are now brought to engage in something altogether different.

I raise these points as a manner of introduction to my thoughts and observations that follow. I hope the progression of analysis makes sense to you, the reader. I start with the killing of the empire because it seems to me that the crux of the entire matter is the loss of empire, the overwhelming debt, the impoverishment of our people against our expectations, and the resulting national drift. My premise is that if we were strong, working hard, and growing, we would sublimate our differences to the positive core. But if the core is hollow, we then begin to chafe at our differences.

I will spend some time discussing our differences that occupy our attention in this era. I won't dwell on them because we know them all so well. I will observe which ones I think (and historians before me have observed) are the salient differences and which ones are red herrings in the debate. The 10 percent are working overtime. Next I will review the debates and events of the 1850s in comparison with more current debates and events so we can evaluate whether that era has relevance to ours.

I will then examine the fraying of our common thread that once bound us together. Finally, we turn to the heart of the matter, searching for the essence of a life worth living in a nation adrift yet determined to bend its citizens to a national behavior norm. I will conclude with speculation on what likely events will occur which lead us to know that we have had the Last Election. And I will suggest what might happen next.

Northwest Michigan

May, 2014

Killing an Empire

America is a great empire, perhaps the greatest empire ever to occupy the earth. Its military prowess is global, dominating nearly all the earth's seas and skies, vastly farther reaching than any empire in history. Its wealth is enormous, both in natural resources, tillable land, manufacturing capability, research facilities, and corporate presence throughout the planet. There has never been anything like it. Empires this great take a long time to die. But die they do. And all die from within.

Historians are well aware of the rise and fall of civilizations. A common theme throughout the scholarly works of the past two thousand years is that there is a noticeable rhythm to the process which is gradual, almost imperceptible to the population and leaders, and inevitable in its march and outcome. We arrive at the state of Alfred E. Neuman, "What—me worry?"[1] It's going to happen, probably not in my lifetime, nothing I can do, so forget about it. We behave as though the knowledge of historians and their exposition of history are of little use to us in the moment and in the predictive.

Confusing the issue for us are those who write history according to their social agenda. All historians are to some degree revisionists because they apply their intellect in a later time allowing for a different perspective. This process is generally useful to our understanding of ourselves, provided that the exercise is intellectually honest. Unfortunately, much of what is presented in our universities is revisionist claptrap passing without criticism among socialist faculties.

Niall Ferguson, the Harvard historian, at the conclusion of his recent work, *Civilization* (2011), discusses the cyclicality of empires and historians' perspectives on the process, questioning the gradual decline into the abyss of history as is the conventional wisdom.

> Yet it is possible that this whole conceptual framework is, in fact, flawed . . . What if history is not cyclical and slow-moving but arrhythmic— sometimes almost stationary, but also capable of violent acceleration? What if historical time is less like the slow and predictable changing of the seasons and more like the elastic time of our dreams? Above all, what if collapse is not centuries in the making but strikes a civilization suddenly, like a thief in the night?[2]

It seems to me that Ferguson is right with respect to some civilizations. The Incas were wiped out quickly by invaders with guns and steel against their bronze. The Mayans died off quickly when they outbred their food supply. Stone Age peoples, including the American

Indians, were no match for modern technology. But these were not empires.

The Roman Empire, Ferguson notes from a more modern reading of history, did not decline and collapse in a "slow burn" as Gibbon's history suggests but occurred in less than thirty years from about 410 to 439.[3] Others would argue, though, quite correctly, I think, that the decay in the civilization from within began much earlier, such that by 406 the society was so weak and decadent that the empire could not defend itself or its culture. The culture was already dead when the society was fractured by outsiders.

A more recent example is the Ottoman Empire. Ferguson asserts that in 1908 with the rise of the young Turks, the empire might still have been reformed and preserved.[4] Within fourteen years, it was gone. The end that came like Ferguson's "thief in the night" perhaps began over 225 years previous with the defeat of the Turks in the Battle of Vienna (1683). Thereafter, the Ottoman Empire began a long period of fragile stability likened to stagnation, followed by the decay of excess spending in the nineteenth century, essentially bankrupting the empire. Other startlingly rapid collapses noted by Ferguson are the British United Kingdom after World War II and the Soviet Union in the 1980s.[5] Ferguson's insight, which is very useful to us, is to watch for key determinants. When they appear, the end comes fast.

In every case of empire that historians have studied, the rise to wealth is attributable to the exploitation of lands and peoples. This activity involves military force, colonization to domesticate the population, and inculcation of the home culture of language, commerce, religion, and rules of behavior. Some did this well, built enormous wealth relative to the age, and lasted hundreds of years. Whatever their model, their behavior changed over some period leading to their decline and disappearance as empire.

Our contemporary interest is in our American Empire and what sorts of behavioral changes are leading us to the Last Election. Again, Ferguson's *Civilization* is useful. His grand theme is to answer the question, what made the West different from the rest of the world. He lists

> "six mainsprings of global power . . . the killer apps—that allowed a minority of mankind originating on the western edge of Eurasia to dominate the world for the better part of 500 years.

> 1. Competition—a decentralization of both political and economic life, which created the launch-pad for both nation-states and capitalism
> 2. Science—a way of studying, understanding and ultimately changing the natural world, which gave the West (among other things) a major military advantage over the Rest.
> 3. Property rights—the rule of law as a means of protecting private owners and peacefully resolving disputes between them, which formed the basis for the most stable form of representative government

4. Medicine—a branch of science that allowed a major improvement in health and life expectancy, beginning in Western societies, but also in their colonies

5. The consumer society—a mode of material living in which the production and purchase of clothing and other consumer goods play a central economic role, and without which the Industrial Revolution would have been unsustainable

6. The work ethic—a moral framework and mode of activity derivable from (among other sources) Protestant Christianity, which provides the glue for the dynamic and potentially unstable society created by apps 1 to 5"[6]

For our purpose in this discussion, these six concepts provide a useful framework to examine current trends in the American society. What, if any, fundamental changes in our behavior are occurring, and when did they start? Consider the following observations on three of Ferguson's "six killer apps" as examples of fundamental changes that have occurred in America over the past eighty years. These changes do not auger well for the empire.

Competition

The nature of competition in America today is far different from a time eighty-four years ago on the eve of the Great Depression when the chaotic energy of the free market was perhaps at its peak. Since 1930, the national political power has become an ever increasing presence in the marketplace. One could argue that the process began earlier with the passage of the Sherman Act to control the huge business trusts that were monopolizing industries, or the National Railway Labor Act.

Perhaps a more appropriate moment was the juxtaposition of the passage of the Smoot-Hawley Tariff and the Great Crash. The House passed the tariff bill in May 1929, and the Senate debated the measure until the spring of 1930. Some assert that the stock market crash in October 1929 was due in no small part to the pending tariff bill. The tariff essentially placed a 60 percent tax on the import of over 3,200 products across a wide swath of the American economy. Trading partners reacted with their own tariffs, adversely affecting a similarly large swath of the economy's products moving to export markets.[7]

The inclination of the central political power to regulate national economic activity has grown exponentially over the past eight decades to include nearly every facet from agriculture to banking, from securities markets to security providers, labor relations, product safety, health care, recreational activity, energy production, transportation, and on and on and on. There is no form of economic activity today that is not touched by the Central Authority of national government. The corner dry-cleaner family of immigrants is regulated by OSHA and EEOC, to name just two central bureaucracies enforcing national laws affecting their economic activity.

The control of economic activity and competition among participants during this eighty-year period has slowly morphed from a perceived need by the central government to assure the orderliness of economic activity to the perceived need to direct economic activity to achieve socially (politically) desirable outcomes. The latter form has always been present, often with a positive result for the nation. What has changed is the pervasiveness of the Central Authority's reach across the entire economic spectrum, which has come to us in three large waves during the mid-1930s, mid-1960s, and following the crash of 2008. The Central Authority now accounts for over 50 percent of GNP if one applies a modest economic multiplier to actual expenditures. The trend to Central Authority has at least three significant consequences.

First, those engaged in economic activity tend to need much larger organizations to be able to afford the lobbyists and other influencers of Central Authority decision making. The big have to get bigger to be effective, not just in global competition but in understanding how to take advantage of what the Central Authority is directing and to pay the millions of dollars (billions total) for access to these officials.

The nation's core financial structure, commercial banks, has been concentrated dramatically into the hands of the very few, who have been allowed to grow much larger so that the Central Authority can justify increasing control through expansion of the rules to "protect" us from their systemic risk. Since 1985, a span of less than twenty years, the number of federally insured banks declined 62 percent from 18,000 to

6,891. Sixteen banks now control over 50 percent of deposits of 166 million Americans on the East and West Coasts. Between the two coasts, where 47 percent of Americans live on 75 percent of the land mass of the lower forty-eight states, the number of banks that control over 50 percent of the people's deposits has shrunk 67 percent in just ten years from 130 to 53.[8] The ever-increasing reach and intensity of federal banking regulation is driving concentration, which in turn drives the justification for more intense federal control. Smaller banks cannot survive the regulatory onslaught.

The second significant consequence of a huge Central Authority is that the source of economic instability is now the Central Authority itself rather than the chaos of the marketplace. The crash of 2008 is directly tied to the political demands to provide housing for millions of citizens who could not afford the loans but were granted them because two federal agencies were guaranteeing them. The enterprise driven by Congress became so enormous, these loans had to be packaged and sold abroad. The financiers made huge sums facilitating the wishes of the Central Authority, and many more thousands were employed to build the houses. Those raising the warning flags were shouted down by the Central Authority. The marketplace could never have created this chaos. Only a central political authority could do so. A decade earlier, the dot-com bubble was the direct result of the development by the Central Authority of the Internet, a brand-new free marketplace that spawned thousands of businesses that were unsustainable.

The third significant consequence is that the pervasiveness of the Central Authority slows the pace of economic activity to that of the least efficient common denominator. The timeline for approval of permits and licensing from the Central Authority for creation of a vast array of new products or construction projects in highly regulated industries is determined by the slowest, least efficient, or most stubborn or uncooperative bureaucrat in the process. If the permitting process for a nuclear energy plant is a minimum of fifteen years, how much of this economic activity will occur? Since 1974, nearly forty years previous to this writing, the answer is zero.[9]

We have, in essence, exchanged the chaos and energy of the free marketplace with a Central Authority to channel economic activity among the favored few who grease its palm. Competition is no longer in the free marketplace, but rather in the halls of the Central Authority where contracts, rules, and laws are bought by the highest bidder. The sluggish economic recovery since 2008, the worst in our history, may indicate that we have crossed the tipping point in excess economic regulation and Central Authority diktat.

Property Rights and the Rule of Law

Notions of property rights and freedom of the individual were hotly debated in the late seventeenth and eighteenth centuries in Europe as the first wave of colonists reached the shores of America. In England, property rights were secure through the rule of law. But few held property. The extension of the right to own property to any free white male in the new world of America created the incentive for men and families to risk the voyage and the hardships. Men and couples with no resources came as indentured servants with the knowledge that when freed of their obligation, they too could strive to own property.

We learned over the next three hundred years that the incentive to better one's material station and protect it is the most powerful catalyst to sustainable human effort. This emotion in excess is described as greed and can be destructive. But it is far preferable to the unsustainable emotional catalysts of fear, lust, and anger. We formed governments to provide civil order to protect our property and our persons. With human energy thus released, we needed rules to resolve disputes among the participants.

The rule of law is effective if the following three criteria are met: (1) the making of rules is performed in a manner supported by the consent of those subject to them, (2) rules of behavior are known and understandable to the participants, and (3) rules are enforced by delegated authority in a systematic, unbiased, and competent regimen. The American experiment has never succeeded in meeting these criteria, but its endeavor has been to succeed, and that effort, more than any other success, has sustained the nation to date.

The building and sustaining of an empire under an effective rule of law requires a fourth criterion be met: (4) rules are formulated and enforced to facilitate economic activity. The industrial revolution required more laws to maintain order in the face of much more robust economic activity. By the late nineteenth century, states and the national government had adopted numerous laws to facilitate the rapid growth of commerce among the states. Commercial and consumer activity was no longer limited to local or even regional materials and transactions. Consumers were purchasing products from catalogues with no knowledge of the producers, the products, or reputations except by the advertisement in the catalogue. Rules were developed to facilitate this commerce to assure buyers that they could rely on the information provided.

Until the mid-1930s, rules were made by passing laws in the legislatures and by courts in deciding individual cases of dispute. In 1932, there was no Federal Register of rules and proposed rules to be issued under umbrella laws passed by the national government. That process began with the first wave of Central Authority lawmaking over banking, securities, labor, food, and drugs that created permanent government agencies (also called commissions) to oversee these sectors of the economy. These commissions were authorized to make rules on their own. The Federal Register was created in 1935 to serve as the notice publisher of proposed rules and new final rules. The first issue of the Federal Register was published March 16, 1936. It contained eleven (11) pages. During the remainder of 1936, an additional 2,609 pages were published, as the newly created federal agencies began making rules. In 1937, Congress approved the need to codify all the new rules being issued. The Code of Federal Regulations (known as CFR) was created in October 1938. The table below summarizes the growth in the Federal Register and the CFR since inception.[10]

	Federal Register		Number of Pages Published Code of Federal Regulations	
Year	Annual	Weekly Ave.	Annual Total	New Regulations
1937	3,450	66	*	
1947	8,902	171	*	
1957	11,156	215	*	
1967	21,088	406	*	
1977	65,603	1,262	84,729	84,297
1987	49,654	955	114,337	113,415
1997	68,530	1,318	131,060	130,112
2007	74,408	1,431	156,010	150,752
2011	82,415	1,585	169,301	160,757

Source: National Archives published data
*   Not available on Archives published data website

The growth spikes in rules governing economic and social behavior parallel the three great waves in legislation during the mid-thirties, mid-sixties, and the 2008-10 period. The numbers will increase dramatically when the banking legislation and the national health care legislation rules are promulgated in the 2013-15 period, mirroring the dramatic increase following the Great Society legislation in the sixties.

Perhaps more useful to our inquiry is to observe the steady growth in rules over the past seventy-five years. The rate of growth may increase or decline dramatically depending on the activism of political parties in power, but the growth occurs notwithstanding. Also of note is that existing rules are modified nearly every year. In 2011 the CFR contained a total of 169,301 pages, of which 160,757 (95 percent) were new or amended regulations.

To provide a point of common reference, the New International Version, large print edition, of the Holy Bible contains 1,939 pages. The Code of Federal Regulations is eighty-seven Bibles, of which eighty-three Bibles are amended annually. The Federal Register will soon be publishing a new bible each week for the American people to study for its effects on their economic activity.

The thousands of pages of new rules and amendments to rules require people employed to write them, many more people employed to influence the writing for their own private or public interest, and many, many more people employed to read, interpret, and comply with them. During the twenty-two-year period of 1989 to 2011, when the Federal Register increased its annual pages by 30,746 (61 percent) and the CFR increased its annual pages of new or amended rules by 40,361 (34 percent), the number of lawyers increased by 499,873 men and women, a jump of 69 percent. During that same period, the number of lawyers in the District of Columbia increased 83 percent to 50,440.[11]

During the eighty years since the election of 1932, there has been a fundamental change in the rules governing the broad spectrum of economic activity. The sheer number of new rules and annual amendments to those rules at the Central Authority level is simply staggering. And what is even more fundamentally changed is the enormous growth of rule-making authorities that are independent of the legislative process, having been granted the status of an "independent agency." In many cases, perhaps nearly all cases, the mission of these agencies is not to facilitate commerce but to restrict and restrain economic activity to further social goals embodied in the umbrella legislation or conceived within the agency as sufficiently related to its umbrella function. In short, the rule of law as applied by the Central Authority has become a tool to restrain human freedom rather than to facilitate its exercise.

Fundamentally it seems that we are still about the adherence to the rule of law, even though we are coming dangerously close to breach in our official behavior toward our Constitution when its limitations frustrate political initiatives, in our temptation to take property for political purpose dressed up as public purpose, and in our politically biased and selective enforcement of certain laws to intimidate disfavored private citizens and institutions. We have lived with corrupt official behavior of this sort for the duration of our republic. However, with the concentration of power in the Central Authority, the prospect for mischief reflecting fundamental change is much more likely. Nor can our empire be sustained under the burden of our Central Authority's insatiable addiction to the promulgation of new rules.

The Work Ethic

The work ethic is linked historically and culturally to the rise of Protestant Christianity in the West. Ferguson notes in his chapter on work that "religion matters." Indeed, we will observe later in this book that the Bible matters. Ferguson has it dead right when he writes, "For most of history men had worked to live. But the Protestants lived to work."[12]

My father (1908-2000) had no uncertainties about the importance of work. A good man had to have work. A man without work was a bum. He displayed over his dresser a needlepoint phrase attributed to the Pennsylvania Dutch, "Seems the harder I work the luckier I get." Great empires are built on hard work and lots of it over lifetimes. Historically these empires were built on the backs of slave labor or serf labor of vanquished peoples. The American empire came into its greatness after the Civil War and was built largely by free men and women working to build a better life for themselves and their families. There was to be sure, much exploitation of men, women, and children of all ethnic and racial backgrounds. But there was also something very different about this empire on the North American continent. Immigrants came here by the millions to free themselves from shackles and work as free men and women for a better life.

This was almost entirely a white European population of Protestants, Catholics, and Jews that accepted the mantle of hard work as the warm coat of a free man. Freedom and work were of a piece, indivisible. With freedom came the obligation to work.

The obligation to work was the price of freedom. Freedom was so joyously precious because it was earned through hard work—and if necessary, a man's lifeblood.

The Great Depression came like a fist punch in the stomach of the work ethic. It took the breath away, sapped the energy, and humiliated the working man. World War II provided an escape from this now stagnant economy, and those that returned once again had work to rebuild and feed the world destroyed by war. But then something untoward began to work its way into our society that reflects a fundamental change in the way we think about ourselves.

Those of us who work are working fewer hours, and there is a smaller percentage of us working who are of working age. Charles Murray describes this change in his recent *Coming Apart* (2012), a statistical analysis comparing several aspects of life in the white population in America during the fifty years from 1960 to 2010. Focusing on prime age white males ages thirty to forty-nine, he notes that most are working. Only 8 percent are out of the work force in 2004-2008, but that number is more than three times the percentage that were out of the workforce in 1960-64.[13] In 1960, Murray observes that the head of household worked a full-time job in 90 percent of white-collar homes and 81 percent of blue-collar homes, but by 2008 before the recession hit, white-collar homes still had an 87 percent rate, but the blue-collar community had dropped to 60 percent. By 2010, white-collar was still at 87 percent and blue-collar had dropped to 53 percent.[14]

Looking at the broader workforce, in 1972 the participation of men in the labor force under age sixty-five was 91 percent, according to data published by the Census Bureau and the Bureau of Labor Statistics. By 2010, the percentage had dropped to 84 percent. In 1972, there were six million men under sixty-five who were not participating in the labor force. By 2010, the number had increased 167 percent to sixteen million. In just ten years between 2000 and 2010, the number of males over sixty-five increased five million, but the number of males dropping out of the workforce increased fourteen million. In addition, in 2010, there were 8.6 million men looking for work but unemployed. Twenty-five million men of working age not working. This number is over 25 percent of the non-institutionalized civilian male population.[15]

Growth in food stamp entitlement is a stark example of change in our society. In 1974, a decade after the initiation of the program in the Great Society legislation, about fourteen million Americans received food stamp assistance, or about 6.5 percent of the civilian population. In 2012, the number had grown to nearly forty-seven million Americans, about 15.4 percent of the household population.[16] Food stamp entitlement did not drop when unemployment eased in 2010-2012 and is not expected to drop materially in coming years as both the federal government and several states have expanded eligibility for this federal program.

Not surprisingly, the decline in workforce participation is symptomatic of changes in attitudes. Mr. Murray reports that attitudes toward work changed dramatically from 1973 to 2006, citing GSS surveys in which respondents claimed less interest in having important work that gave them a feeling of accomplishment and much more interest in a job with shorter work hours and no danger in being fired.[17] Murray also reported data from the Social Security Administration showing an 800 percent increase in people on disability benefits from 0.7 percent of the labor force in 1960 to 5.3 percent of the labor force in 2010.[18] Even this leap in percentages understates the gravity of the change. In 1960, the total number would have been about eight hundred thousand people. In 2010, that number would have grown to 12.6 million people, nearly sixteen times greater. This, despite forty years of work life under OSHA regulation and less strenuous physical labor required in nearly all jobs.

The dramatic rise in the number of people on disability has not gone unnoticed in the general population. A popular story circulating on the Internet has a car salesman telling of a woman applying for credit to buy a new Ford Focus while on disability saying she is doing better than when she was working. She used to take home about $330 per week, but now she gets a $1,500 monthly government check, $700 per month on an EBT food stamp card, and $800 for rent, plus the 250 free minutes on her cell phone. "Do the math," the storyteller urges, "and then ask yourself why the hell should she go back to work." Whether or not this tale is true, the story has credence, and its popularity reflects a growing unease with trends in our society.

In 2013, the Cato Institute published a sequel to its 1995 study on work and welfare.[19] Total welfare program benefits in all fifty states were analyzed (126 separate federal antipoverty programs). The pretax equivalent of combined welfare payments in thirty-three states and the District of Columbia beats by a wide margin the higher minimum wage of $10.10 proposed by the president in his 2014 budget. In twenty-seven states, it exceeds $12 per hour. In most states, welfare pays better than the starting wage of an office secretary. In half the states, benefits exceed the federal poverty level by 150 percent to 221 percent, with the District of Columbia being the highest. In seven East Coast states plus Hawaii, welfare pays more pretax than the median salary. In those states, over 50 percent of the working people are earning less than their neighbor who is not working and on welfare.

What happened to the work ethic? Since the Great Society legislation in the mid-1960s, we have become slowly but steadily a nation of rights, principally rights to receive care from our Central Authority, beginning with prenatal care, infant care, day care, preschool, primary, secondary, and college subsidies for the young. If one is a citizen or even an illegal alien, one is entitled to the benefits provided by the Central Authority. As the number of benefits has increased over nearly a half century, the ethic of work as an obligation has receded. If I can get a roof over my head (rent subsidy stipend), food (food stamps), health care (Medicaid), and clothing (welfare check), will I do labor for small wages, take other work I don't like or is inconvenient, or feel the need to just be working as a way of life? Maybe I would, but the numbers show that many of us now wouldn't.

Go back for a moment to the twenty-five million men not working. If our society is supporting these men with $25,000 to $30,000 in benefits, including Medicaid health care, the tax on the rest of society is $625,000,000,000 ($625 billion) annually. In 2012, over $541 billion was paid out in benefits to alleviate poverty, not including Medicaid, which was another $308 billion. And for people over age sixty-five, add another $472 billion for Medicare. In 1960, the federal government paid out about $19 billion in income transfers to individuals in current dollars. If we include social security payments, the total income transfer in 2012 was $2.1 trillion.[20] But that's not even the worst of it. If these twenty-five million men were working in manufacturing where the ratio of output value to labor input value is at least ten to one at the margin, the gross national product would benefit by over $6 trillion.[21] The opportunity cost to our society, our nation, is simply staggering.

An Empire in Decline

Reflecting on the "six killer apps" listed by Ferguson, much has changed in our America. We have evolved over the past 120 years from a decentralized political and economic life to a highly centralized society in which the Central Authority spends 25 percent of the gross national product, drives over 50 percent of GNP using a modest economic multiplier, and arguably controls through vast regulation of commercial behavior 75 percent or more of the economy. The nation's commercial life has been consolidated over the past twenty-five years into a relative handful of vastly powerful corporations that feed first and foremost off the expenditure of the Central Authority and the protective laws it enacts for their benefit. The national economic structure today looks more like that of the Ming dynasty (top down) than the robust America acting out its Manifest Destiny as a free people.

Our appetite for space exploration has waned. Our astronauts must now use Russian rockets. We developed our empire by control of the seas and the skies. We are now reducing our blue-water navy and disbanding aircraft development. Our pharmaceutical industry is the envy of the planet, but we seem more bent on restraining and taxing it rather than celebrating it.

Our interest in science remains dynamic, but it is constantly harassed and perverted by social agendas that spew junk science for the purpose of political gain. Climate change is a reality that may have an enormous and catastrophic impact on coastal populations, lanes of commerce, and food sources. Yet the inquiry and conversation in scientific circles is characterized mostly by protecting one's turf and one's preconceived social agenda for how we all ought to live. Where is truth to be had?

In the second decade of the twenty-first century, the centralization of power in America resembles more the latter days of the great empires of history than the robust building phases of those empires. It remains to be seen whether our vigor in science and medicine will survive this centralization of authority in a federal government. We do know that the education of our children seems to be more focused on self-esteem than performance in math and science. And we know that our children are performing in these disciplines well down in the pack of nations.

Perhaps the many signs of decline reflect simply a temporary phase in our development as a nation, a pause if you will, to reflect. A majority of Americans seem concerned only with their individual welfare, and they seem relatively unconcerned with the national welfare. What we don't seem to realize is that we have very little time. The seeds of our destruction are already sown.

The Stake in the Heart—Our National Debt

The key determinant that can be observed objectively for empires is money. The rise of an empire brings wealth to the civilization which its people use to maintain power and perpetuate their empire. The decline phase begins with changes in behavior within the population and its rulers which manifest collectively in the end as a lack of cash. Without money or the ability to borrow it, the empire cannot finance its defense, and the collapse follows quickly. Changes in behavior may take numerous forms, but these changes have the common theme of behavior markedly different from and inconsistent with the behavior norms prevailing during the rise of the empire.

We have looked briefly at three major changes in behavior of the American people inconsistent with empire building according to the thinking of Ferguson in *Civilization*: (1) demand for less work and more rights, (2) less freedom of action and more rules, and

(3) less appetite for competition in the marketplace and more yearning for central control. But we have not examined the behavior of the Central Authority itself.

Seeing behavioral changes in a stable government and assessing them is not so simple a task. One is left with the question after visiting Versailles, "What were they thinking?" The ridiculous excess of opulence (a redundancy is called for here) is so outrageously obvious, one can only conclude that this society was headed for a fall. Yes, but to what are we comparing Versailles in French history of government? Is this edifice the result of a behavioral change in the culture or simply a very French expression of how the good life in a prominent society should be lived?

A more useful example is to compare the two Ottoman Empire palaces in Istanbul. Topkapi Palace on Sultanahmet was built on the high bluff overlooking the Bosphorus and the Golden Horn, served by the Roman aqueduct and cistern. Its structures are all about the business of administering to the growing empire, defending the city, and being able to survive a siege. It reflects the serious work of building and administering to an empire. It was built shortly after the conquest of Constantinople in 1453 and was the home of the sultans and seat of government for nearly four hundred years. Dolmabahce Palace on the Bosphorus was built during a thirteen-year period 1843-1856 and reflects the rulers' desire to express opulence in the midst of a decaying empire. Whereas Topkapi is characterized by indigenous tiles and Ottoman carving, Dolmabahce is European in architecture with fourteen tons of gold leaf ceilings and enormous displays of crystal in chandeliers and staircases. It is trying to be Versailles East. It fails.

More importantly, the Dolmabahce reflects a marked change in Turkish cultural behavior from that of the empire builder to that of the empire enjoyer. One behavior creates more wealth than it takes. The other takes more wealth than it creates. We can see the marked change in behavior of the culture from the builders' palace to the decadents' palace. But could the people of the land at the time see this change? Doesn't the change, or in fact the many changes, that are reflected in these two structures, happen so slowly over so many years, in this case four centuries, so as to be imperceptible in contemporary life? One can argue that we can evaluate Dolmabahce, as opposed to Versailles, only because we know Topkapi. And then is it possible, having seen Dolmabache upon completion and the government behavior in residence there, and knowing Topkapi, the Turks could know the end was not far off? Didn't the Young Turks know for sure well before WWI? Of course they did. Mustafa Kemal Ataturk and his men at Gallipoli were fighting for their homeland, not for the empire or the sultanate. They knew the empire was long lost a century or more previous.

Has our federal government materially changed its behavior over the past fifty years that we can see clearly enough to draw any useful parallel to previous empires? Surely we have our excesses that we can lament as the politicians and bureaucrats spend lavishly on travel junkets and ignore the rules required of the rest of us. Yet one would be hard-pressed to argue successfully that our empire is in peril due to the frivolity of government officials wasting our assets on silly expenditures. Yes, our leaders have failed us in two important respects. First, they led us into three wars we did not win. Second, they have not led us to any solutions to our mounting debt. But our leaders are not killing the empire. We are. As Pogo famously uttered, "We have met the enemy and he is us."[22] We are the problem because we are spoiled rotten, and we still believe we are untouchable.

The wealth of America is so vast as to be nearly incomprehensible. We do not have the problem of the Turks whose wealth was ultimately measured in the gold they could accumulate and spend. We can print gold which we call dollars. The dollar has been the reserve currency of the world. Its supply is inexhaustible, at least in the short run. We could freely spend more than we earn or take in because the world has wanted to lend us their money and hold our debt to repay them in dollars. That has now changed. Over the past decade the European currency, the Euro, has become and remains more valuable than the dollar even though the European economies are arguably much weaker.

Recently (since 2009) our Central Bank has been printing dollars, giving them to the US government, who is transferring them to high marginal consumption people (unemployed or not employed) to spend on consumer goods and services. So now the Federal Reserve Bank holds trillions of dollars of US debt that will never be repaid. The Federal Reserve has been printing dollars to support 80 percent of the federal deficit, over $1 trillion per year at virtually no cost in interest. The other 20 percent is being bought by the market. When I asked the chief investment officer of a major Midwest bank in the summer of 2012 how long this could go on, he replied, "Until the other 20% stops buying."

Can anyone seriously argue that the Federal Reserve Bank is behaving irresponsibly when the American people have consistently voted in national elections to keep and increase their entitlements? If Congress and the president won't take away the entitlements and cannot or will not seize by law the assets of the people in taxes, fees, and other confiscatory methods to pay for these entitlements, what other course is there but to print money? Blaming the Central Authority for the mess we created by our childish demands for "our fair share" in entitlements is a fool's errand.

The prevailing view is that there is no consequence because we have no noticeable inflation in the core consumer price index which is constantly being modified to produce benign numbers. We do, of course, have significant inflation occurring in America. All the inflation is in productive assets and, to some degree, protective assets such as gold and gems.

When economists begin measuring the inflation that is actually occurring, the lie will be exposed to the markets. Currently, in America we are printing $1 trillion per year and transferring it to Americans who have a 100 percent plus marginal rate of consumption with zero or negative savings. This $1,000,000,000,000 of newly printed money is spent on food, clothing, housing, medical care, and other essential goods and services provided by Americans who own and employ assets to produce these consumable items. These productive Americans earn a profit, pay their taxes, and save the remainder which earns nothing in the bank as idle cash or in low-risk bonds. Yet there is no incentive to put the money to use in their productive business assets because there is no material growth in demand. There is slight demand growth from a portion of the savings from productive assets, probably in the 1 percent to 1.5 percent range, but not enough to have any macroeconomic effect. Instead there is simply a static demand funded by a trillion dollars of new money to keep the unemployed and underemployed in a subsistence status.

During the period 2008-2011, the money sat in cash as the productive Americans waited for clearer signals. None came. Finally, the money had to go into something positive, so it has been going into farmland, commercial real estate selectively, and the stock market. Earnings growth in the US does not justify the current market multiples. Neither does earnings growth in Europe. Values in the public markets for corporate shares are inflated by money chasing a productive home. Farm commodity earnings do not justify the prices of farmland. The only justification is the lack of other good alternatives. There is no consumer inflation because the consumer has no money. The money is all held by the productive sector which is now relatively small and consumes selectively.

This dangerous charade can continue for some time. The theory is that we will break out of this treadmill when the economy begins growing at the historically expected pace. The growth may occur in nominal dollars as inflated assets begin to create the false impression of increased wealth which would support an increase in purchases of discretionary goods and services whose prices also will rise to meet the demand. But the bottom half, or by this time perhaps 60 or 70 percent of the American people, will remain in survival mode, preventing any real growth or measurable real wealth creation.

In late 2013, the Federal Reserve indicated it would begin to reduce the amount of money it was printing each month to indirectly support the federal deficit spending. As the Fed tapers the amount it is contributing, the US Treasury will have to borrow more from independent lenders both here and abroad. Interest rates will rise, replacing asset inflation with real inflation and further debilitating the federal government by dramatically increasing its interest rate burden. The Federal Reserve is committed to low interest rates for the economy through at least 2015, but it cannot control the cost of US debt on the open market. It can keep the nominal cost of the federal debt in check only by printing money. In any case, until the US government is capable of reducing its spending dramatically, the entire working population of America will get poorer every month.

While economists and pundits seem confused about the lack of any real economic recovery since the so-called end of the recession in 2009, there is no confusion among the general population. In the winter of 2013-2014 after a modest holiday selling season, the economy went back into a virtual no-growth mode in January and February 2014. The weather was blamed, but the results were similar in fair-weather regions. The reason is simple. All but the very wealthy hunkered down after the holidays to pay their bills. The people have no money and are getting poorer as they see their taxes and health-care premiums rise. And the people sense that a very big bill is going to be coming due as our national debt soars unchecked past the $17,000,000,000,000 mark. (That's seventeen trillion dollars!)

The end game for our society arrives when our productive assets, just like our productive labor thirty years ago, becomes overvalued in relation to the rest of the world. Our money is devalued and our asset values crash. We cannot support economic, military, or social activity outside our border. We become Argentina. Does America want to become Argentina? Or Italy or Greece? None of these nations can defend themselves or their economies from predators.

How much longer will it take for us to reach the precipice? No one knows for sure. The Ottoman Empire began to stagnate after the defeat in the Battle of Vienna in 1683 but did not complete its decline to dissolution until the end of World War I, some 235 years later. America began to change its behavior beginning with the social programs of the New Deal in the 1930s, but it did not begin to stagnate until the early 1970s with the implementation of Great Society programs, the defeat in Vietnam, wage-price controls, and the onset of stagflation. We are only into this growing malaise some forty years. It would seem we have a long way to go. But maybe not. Great Britain survived but did not win two devastating wars and lost its empire in the span of forty years from 1914 through 1954, giving up ten colonies to independence in the decade following World War II.

During the Ottoman decline in the eighteenth and nineteenth centuries, armies and commerce moved at a walk and horse-drawn carriage. Today movement is several orders of magnitude faster. Communication and response required weeks and months. Today we measure in hours and days. Information was outdated before receipt. Now it is real-time sent and received. It is not much of a stretch to suggest that the pace of both decline and ascendancy to power and influence has quickened by a significant multiple, possibly as high as ten. The Soviet Empire rose dramatically following WWII and collapsed within forty years. If it were not for our vast wealth and military might, together with our status as the world's reserve currency, we might by now be over the precipice.

Our republic has withstood countless challenges and difficulties during our now fairly significant history. We are no longer a young nation by any standards. Nor are we immature in our culture and worldliness. Over the past sixty odd years since World War II, we have become soberly adult in our behavior, accepting the burden of world leader and keeper of order. We have fought three wars, lost one hands down, and will be said to have lost the other two in time. We can no longer insure the peace. We have become more reluctant in the role demanded of us by our allies and are even wistful for less responsibility in the affairs of others. We had the strength and resolve to outlast the threat of Communism, but we are left exhausted, much like Great Britain after World War II. In short, we seem to be getting ready for the fall.

Had we won the wars of the past fifty years and ruthlessly taken the spoils available to us, maybe we could afford our vast promises to our people. But, alas, we have lost these wars, spent trillions of our national wealth, crippled and killed our citizen soldiers, and wasted our power. History is unkind to civilizations that lose wars. None has survived. Empires don't recede. They die. The civilization that comprises the empire shrinks to some other mode entirely and often disappears from the pages of history.

America has vast wealth, more than any other empire in history. Yet this wealth is dependent for its value and maintenance on commercial activity across the globe, which in turn is wholly dependent on a big blue-water navy that dominates the seas together with an untouchable air force that commands the skies. Our armed forces are bloated and bureaucratic, General Motors writ large. Where we desperately need excellence, we find mediocrity and a dearth of leadership. It should be obvious to anyone that many of the characteristics of our success are now being emulated by our global competitors. Per capita GDP ratios are narrowing and beginning to overlap. China is developing its navy supported by vast resources.

The path forward for America will be much more difficult as we operate in a more competitive world. Arguably, we must be stronger now than ever before. Yet we feel weaker. Our rivals will overcome us due not to their strength but to our own weakness, much in the way we prevailed as we built our empire over our weaker rivals. Ferguson appears clearly alarmed by America's decline, reminding us once again, "It is historians who retrospectively portray the process of dissolution as slow-acting, with multiple over-determining causes. Rather, civilizations behave like all complex adaptive systems. They function in apparent equilibrium for some unknowable period. And then, quite abruptly, they collapse."[23]

Divided We Stand

We are now a deeply divided nation. We all know this because our national media inform us, our national elections inform us, our union halls inform us, our churches inform us, our educational institutions inform us, and bookstores are crowded with new releases on our disunity. Are we just going through another phase of change, or is something more fundamental occurring in our midst? The answer to that question will likely bear on the title to this book.

The divisions among us are so pervasive and incessantly broadcast over our national media, it is a daunting task to try to make sense of it all. Yet make sense of it we must if we are to avoid impoverishment, remain a relatively free people, and conduct our lives according to our personal preferences for living.

The Specter of Impoverishment

As a nation and a people, we are going broke. Our federal government is insolvent (it cannot meet its obligations as they come due), so it is printing money to fund itself and, incredible as it may seem, fund further growth every year. We are not yet bankrupt because our assets (namely, great land masses and mineral reserves) still exceed our liabilities. But unless we want to sell Hawaii or Alaska, for example, we have no means to honor our stated obligations to ourselves and to others who own our debt. This statement is not hyperbole. It is reality. It is no less real because we choose to ignore it.

Unfunded Promises to Promised Classes

Since the 1930s we have made many, many promises to our people to care for them in need and in old age. Until the adoption of Medicare in the late 1960s, we funded these obligations as we went along. However, we did not fund Medicare. We asserted at the time that Medicare would be a tiny expenditure in the federal budget. This forecast proved terribly wrong, but we nevertheless refused to fund it, and instead we drew upon the Social Security Trust Fund to pay the expenses. Evidently we really liked this method of governing, so we proceeded to make many more promises without providing the means to pay for them. Now these promises are breaking us.

Anger and fear are running rampant through every community in our nation, always flowing just below the surface, and often boiling over the top to hit the front page of the newspaper. There is one common denominator to it all—enormous unfunded promises that we are now unable or unwilling to honor. There are two sets of promised classes in America. The first set can be defined broadly as those in need. The second set can be defined broadly as those retired from government service.

Those in Need

Annual payments to Americans in need mushroomed from $19 billion in 1960 to $2.2 trillion in 2013, a dramatic 114 fold increase. In 1960 the total represented 21 % of the federal budget. The total now represents 62% of the budget. The breakdown in major segments is as follows:

	Fiscal 2013
Income Security (social security and welfare)	$1,314,000,000,000
Medicare	472,000,000,000
Medicaid	308,000,000,000
SNAP (food stamps)	79,900,000,000
Total	$2,173,900,000,000

Sources: OMB and SNAP data

Those Americans in need include the unemployed, disabled, working poor, retired persons over 65 years of age and their survivors. In 2013 there were 48 million retired and survivors receiving social security. In addition there were 57 million Americans under age 65 in poverty according to data published by the Kaiser Family Foundation. If we assume that the 11 million Americans receiving disability checks, the 48 million Americans receiving food stamps, the 8.3 million receiving supplemental security income and the 3 plus million collecting unemployment compensation are included in the 57 million estimated to be living in poverty, the total number of Americans in need is approximately 105 million, or roughly one third of our population.

Caring for this many Americans in need is not possible. The social security fund is exhausted. Americans working for a living must support those in need with their earnings. Consider this stark reality. Only 155 million Americans, less than 63% of the non-institutionalized population of working age, are in the work force. Of this number approximately 10 million are unemployed, leaving 145 million actually working. Of this group, approximately 19 million are working only part time, and may indeed be in the group receiving income support from the government.

Thus, there are 126 million Americans working full time. These working Americans are supporting another 90 million children and spouses who are not in the workforce. It is not a stretch to assume that at least 10% of these men and women working full time are at or near the level of working poor, especially if they are trying to support a family. It seems highly likely that there is less than one American working at a living wage for every American in need receiving life support from the federal government.

Income taxes paid by these Americans earning a living wage are woefully insufficient to support an equal or greater number of Americans who are not working, or working part time, and in need. The federal government must print huge sums of dollars to provide for those in need. This state of affairs, though clearly unsustainable, will not change. Of this huge number of people in need, less than 10% are in the workforce and unemployed. The other 90% are likely to be with us for the rest of their lives as persons in need.

Pensions and Benefits

The second set of promised classes are those citizens who have worked for governments (city, county, state, and federal) and are due retirement pensions and other benefits. The unfunded liabilities to these citizens are also staggeringly enormous. The federal government's unfunded liability to federal employees was $762 billion in 2011, up $139 billion from the year before. The nation's fifty states were underfunded to their employees in 2011 by over $3.4 trillion on pension obligations and other retirement benefits, including health care. The nation's sixty-one largest cities were underfunded on obligations to their employees by $217 billion as of 2009 for pension and retirement health benefits.

What's even worse is that the known unfunded aggregate liability of $4.379 trillion is clearly understated. Actuaries estimate the liability based on life expectancies and promised plan payments. The amount of assets required to fund those estimated payments over the coming years is the funding requirement. A fully funded plan would have sufficient assets today to pay out its obligations over time. The key subjective variable is the assumed rate of return the plan assets will earn annually to augment the plan funds. Governments routinely overestimate the prospective investment returns on plan funds. Therefore, the actual level of unfunded obligations is an order of magnitude greater than the $4.4 trillion acknowledged. These obligations are on top of an estimated $7.3 trillion of combined debt issued by state and local governments.

Public Class versus Private Class

Our fellow citizens in need and due pensions and benefits on retirement will be impoverished when the money is not there for them. We can try to reduce these obligations, but we face strong civil unrest with every attempt to do so.

Of the working population of approximately 145 million people, about 24 million or 17 percent work for government at the local, state, and federal level. The rate of labor unionization in the public sector in 2012 was 36 percent compared to only 7 percent in the private sector. Public unions have succeeded because they are powerfully effective in winning elections and negotiating with bureaucrats and politicians. As a result, today public wages exceed private wages for comparable work, and benefits for retirement and health care far outstrip those in the private sector.

Private unions were even more powerful than public unions in 1960, but in the ensuing fifty years, the unions effectively (and unintentionally) drove entire industries into bankruptcy including steel, autos, and airlines to cite a few. Other industries moved offshore to survive. Our manufacturing base has dwindled, and the number of union workers (dues paying members) has likewise dwindled, leaving less money for political action and influence. Moreover, the benefits accruing from private union membership have declined dramatically as wages have flattened or even declined, pension plans have moved to defined contribution from defined benefit, and health-care plans are less robust.

We have arrived at the moment in our history when there are fewer workers and less net income in the private sector to support a larger number of public workers promised significantly higher benefits. It is no surprise, then, that all across America, towns, school districts, cities, and states are drowning in debt and out of cash. There are no more reserves. And citizens do not have or are unwilling to provide the resources to fund all these promises. The public sector, like the old unionized private sector, has been far too successful over the past fifty years.

Private sector workers have already suffered huge negative adjustments to their pension and health benefits with the bankruptcies over the past twenty years in the airline, steel, auto, and other industries. There is no sympathy in the private sector for government employees who must also reduce their pension and health benefits. The protests of public union employees, sometimes violent, have not been embraced with solidarity by private sector neighbors. Everyone is coming to know that confrontations lie ahead in every community and state in our land.

Public bankruptcies loom on the horizon and may come in a rush. They may take several forms and will be preceded by months and years of legislative discussion and inaction, prolonging the day of reckoning. Detroit has played out this dance of denial for several years, only now to be forced to confront the reality of no money and $20 billion of obligations. The Illinois legislature simply will not come to a conclusion, excusing their inaction with worries over which solution might be constitutional. What difference does that argument make if there is no money? The market is ruthless with the private economy, but the market does not yet know how to behave in America with the public economy. Thus, the public economy has been allowed to dither longer to its misfortune. This will all come to pass, and when it does, and as it is happening, which is beginning now, we as a people do not know how to deal with this reality.

The public class restructuring is going to be ugly because it will involve millions of citizens who opted for the public vocation in part because of economic certainty. No risk. The brutal reality of misfortune is not only unwelcome but anathema to these citizens' notions of reality. Worse, though, is that unlike the bankruptcies of whole private industries in the past decades in which the victims' fellow citizens observed the fate of their neighbors with benign neglect, in the case of the public bankruptcies and restructurings, the neighbors are voting to refrain from paying the obligations incurred. This is not benign neglect but assertive negation. Witness the Madison, Wisconsin, and Lansing, Michigan, demonstrations to changes in benefits for public employees. These are but the harbinger of more to come.

The big division of the public class and the private class is not whether they can coexist in society but whether they are capable of reconciliation to similar modes of economic risk and outcome. In America we do not have an institutional framework to accomplish this reconciliation because one is driven by market discipline and the other by political power. The twain does not meet here. Thus, as we try to muddle through our failed promises, we have set ourselves up for civil strife of the first order.

Taxes

America has always been divided on taxation. By force of law and arms if necessary, we are required to contribute portions of our earnings and wealth to our community as determined by our elected officials. Complaints over taxation are not any more prevalent today than in the past.

But the issue itself is much more divisive today than in the past due to the looming burden of unfunded promises made by our federal and state governments. Somebody is going to suffer. Will it be the promised classes who will find the cupboard empty and be subjected to abject poverty? Or will it be the productive class whose earnings and savings will be confiscated by government?

The issue is playing itself out in the national conversation as "paying our fair share" or, more demagogically, "paying *your* fair share." What does this mean? Assertions are being made by one side of the divide that the rich are not paying their share, implying that this is a new unfair development from decades-old tax cuts. Yet a recent report reveals that in 1958 (before the Kennedy-era tax cuts), the top 3 percent of taxpayers earned 14.7 percent of all adjusted gross income and paid 29.2 percent of all federal income taxes. In 2010, a half century later, the top 3 percent earned 29.2 percent of income and paid 51 percent of all income taxes.[24] Not much change proportionally. Although rates are flatter, deductions for the high earners have pretty much disappeared and corporate perks are now taxed as income.

The same picture emerges from Tax Policy Center data indicating that in 2010, 54 percent of taxpayers (earning taxable income between $50,000 and $500,000) paid 61 percent of income taxes. Above the $500,000 taxable income level (less than 1 percent of filers), the total paid was over $300 billion, 32 percent of all income tax paid. Those below $50,000, a full 45 percent of all taxpayers, paid 7 percent of all taxes. So the other side of the divide asks, who is not paying their fair share?

Obviously, the real issue is not paying one's fair share. The real taxation issue is grounded in two other factors. First if I am in the promised class, "paying your fair share" means that those who I think are able to pay more must be made to pay more so the promise to me is kept. In 2010, there were an estimated four million taxpayers earning taxable income over $200,000 who paid marginal tax rates of 33-35 percent. Those same taxpayers back in 1960 (adjusting for inflation) would have been paying rates of 47 percent to 91 percent on the same taxable income. The promised classes want that money and will vote for whoever will get it for them.

The second factor involves the 50 percent of taxpayers earning taxable income of $50,000 to

$200,000. They are paying 41 percent of all the income taxes, and none of them think of themselves as rich or even comfortably well off. They know that there are not enough high earners to sate the appetite of the promised classes, which leaves these productive middle earners holding the bag. On the same income in 1960 adjusted for inflation, this group would have been paying 22 percent to 43 percent on their taxable income, whereas in 2010 the flatter rates are 25 percent to 28 percent. Again, though, many more activities were deductible expenses in 1960 and nearly all corporate perks such as cars, clubs, legal services, airplane use, and the like were nontaxable.

Nobody cares about the rich. They can take care of themselves. The real divide in America on taxation is between the great middle class who would like to avoid impoverishment by keeping their savings and the promised classes who wish to avoid impoverishment by getting what the others have.

Printing Money

If Congress won't increase taxes enough to make a dent in the debt load, our national government thinks the way out is to simply print money as we have been doing at the rate of $1.2 trillion per year. The consequences of such behavior are nearly the same. Everyone will have the value of their nominal dollar reduced to a level that assures poverty for nearly everyone. This is happening right now. The first stage is the great reduction in the velocity of money, as the $1.2 trillion of newly printed cash is distributed through federal programs to people with 100 percent marginal consumption rates to fund staying alive. The producers of goods and services maintain a static level of sales, earn some profit, pay taxes, and have a little left over as savings which they do not invest in their businesses because there is no increase in demand. Instead they invest in available productive assets such as farmland and shares of stock in publicly held corporations, creating asset inflation. There is no other source of inflation because 95 percent of Americans have no money, no savings, and live hand to mouth. Stagflation is upon us.

It is amazing to listen to intellectuals on this subject in the American media. Men and women who should know better insist that the Federal Reserve Bank is not printing money. It is buying bonds from banks who are then not lending their increased reserves. Actually, the banks are taking these reserves and buying more government Treasury bills and notes which are issued by the Treasury for the purpose of . . . you guessed it . . . funding the mass distribution of funds to 50 percent of Americans who need it to stay alive. The Federal Reserve plays this shell game because it is prohibited from buying Treasury notes and bills directly from the Federal Treasury who issues them. The Federal Reserve can maintain this charade, forcing the banks to cooperate, because the six or eight largest banks in the United States are so tightly regulated now by the Federal Reserve under our recent laws that these banks dare not cross the Fed lest they be crippled in their operations. The Chinese and other nations are no longer lending us money to fund our deficits. We are funding over 80 percent of our deficits with the printing of money.

If the people are not required to work or live off their savings but are maintained in ever increasing numbers by the printing of money, soon the asset inflation of the past few years will escalate to all consumer goods. It is beginning now with higher value goods and services available to the 5 percent of Americans who have discretionary income and savings. It will soon spread to imported goods and agricultural products as foreign producers will exercise preferences for one currency over the other. At the moment, we take comfort that Europe is a sorrier mess than the United States. Silly us. Printing money is the worst of all government behaviors because it discriminates harshly against the most productive citizens, the most frugal citizens, and the hardest working citizens while favoring with cash the least productive, most profligate, and laziest citizens, thus setting up the citizenry for conflict instead of cooperation in shouldering to the task.

Urban/Rural Divide

Our societal division that can be observed between urban and rural culture has been with us for our entire history as a continuation of that division in Europe. However, the division was not important to our society until the middle of the twentieth century because of two salient factors. First, if one did not wish to opt for the urban culture, there was land aplenty for the taking, so "Go west, young man." Citizens had few possessions, and the decision to pick up stakes and take leave was more about leaving family than it was about hauling possessions, selling one's home, finding a new affordable home, and landing a good job. If urban life was a dead end, there was not much to lose by heading west, and much maybe to gain.

Second, freedom was and remains for many a highly valued state of living, and freedom lay in the open spaces to the west. Perhaps life would be hard work and risky and frankly unrewarding, but to live free in a wide open space to call one's own was a very attractive alternative to urban confinement, soot, foul air, and crime. But by the midtwentieth century, there was little "west" left except in Alaska. The lower forty-eight states have now been settled except for Indian territories and government land. The price of open land today is so high that only movie stars, investment bankers, and rock stars can afford to buy. So for urban dwellers, there is little escape. And for rural America, there is no freedom from EPA, OSHA, EEOC, IRS, and the immigration inspectors. This circumstance now sets us up for a fundamental clash between rural and city folk.

Urban Life Today

City life today is good for the few and dreary for the many. The few enjoy thrilling spectator sports and artistic performances, stimulating competition of the intellect in white-collar dress, food and drink to liven the palate, all with no worry of where the food came from, how the electricity works, or what happens to the sewage.

For the uneducated many, gone are the giant manufacturing and food processing factories of the twentieth century, the high union wages, and pensions that allowed for a cabin in the woods or a boat on a trailer in the yard. That work has gone to smaller cities or offshore to foreign countries. The uneducated urbanite today is performing service work at low wages for the white-collar educated downtown crowd of lawyers, bankers, stock brokers, investment bankers, accountants, marketing professionals, and corporate headquarters administrative staffs.

The urban citizen never had freedom except for the hope of opportunity which for some proved a reality after the waves of immigration from 1870 to 1920. The urban citizen did find community within an ethnic culture and the Catholic Church or synagogue while assimilating the American experience. The urban citizen's life gradually improved until the Great Depression and then again after World War II. Children went to elementary school and eventually to college. Life was good, especially compared to what was left behind.

Since the 1960s, though, life in urban neighborhoods has been in decline. Charles Murray in his recent book, *Coming Apart*, notes dramatic declines in the importance of community life, church life, and moral values such as honesty and desire to work, particularly in lower-class urban neighborhoods. Murray describes the gradual creation of a new lower class, mostly white and mostly urban. However, he concludes that this new lower class is not just white and urban but American across the land and across all racial and ethnic groups.[25]

Service jobs are mostly a dead end and often part-time. The safety net of various welfare handouts from government keeps food on the table and some heat in winter. Life is not good. But for big government programs, life would be abject poverty. For the urban lower class, there is no out. They are stuck. The only action they can take to improve their lives is the ballot box. Vote for politicians who will make sure government provides income, housing, food, and medical care for you.

Rural Life Today

Rural life today offers little freedom from the reach and control of government. Nearly every activity historically associated with the freedom of wide-open spaces is now heavily regulated by government. Hunting and fishing regulation is more about the animals and the fish than about sustaining human life. Farming practices are now wholly regulated by government, from the pesticides and herbicides used to protect crops, rules restricting the use of water to irrigate crops, runoff from land, and percolation in land, rules restricting the use of water from small lakes and creeks designated as navigable by the federal government, forms and procedures for hiring and retaining farm labor, rules restricting the transportation of crops, rules restricting the fencing of land to protect crops from wild game, rules restricting the cultivation of farmers' land designated as wetlands, rules regulating the storage and housing of chemicals . . . to frankly cite only a few restrictions on farmers.

Without the compensation of a life relatively free of intrusion by government, rural life becomes unattractive unless one can earn a good living comparable to the more crowded city life. In the first place, farming is very hard work. Finding men and women who embrace hard work has become more and more difficult with each succeeding generation since 1960. Farming can be profitable and rewarding if the operation is large enough to finance compliance with all the rules. Farms are getting larger to cope with the scale of government regulation, felt not only directly but indirectly by the farms' food processing customers who are heavily regulated. As a result, many sons and daughters of farming families are forced to sell the farms when the parents pass away. Those who stay are getting bigger of necessity to cope and also to offer sufficient reward for a life of hard work.

Bright, well-educated young men and women from rural upbringing can migrate to cities to seek careers in the professions and other white-collar managerial work. But the great majority, not unlike the great majority in urban life, are not mobile because they lack learning and lack skills. They are stuck in the countryside, working in local shops, food processing plants, and local factories for wages that have little upside and in jobs with little prospect for promotion.

So now here we are. Except for the few who are mobile, we are either stuck in rural or urban/suburban. We are not happy. And our unhappiness is similar among all races and ethnic groups. In *Coming Apart*, Murray cites GSS data for white working-class families and for all working-class families which track very closely from 1970 to 2010, with happiness declining from the 35 percent range in prime-age adults to the 16 percent range.[26] The data presented by Murray clearly shows that the happiness index has historically been highly dependent on work satisfaction, marriage, social trust, and weekly worship, all of which have declined significantly during the past forty years.

Rural people do not "bowl alone" but socialize at church and with family. And yes, there are bowling leagues in rural life. Rural people socialize "religiously" at Friday night high school football games and nearly all other high school sports events, plays, and other events involving their children and their nieces and nephews and grandchildren. Urban people do very little of any of this. Much of urban social life is virtual or anonymous spectator events. Family is less important or nonexistent. Social relationships run a broad spectrum of sexual, racial, religious, and economic preferences.

There is virtually no cultural connection between rural and urban. Even in Michigan Stadium in Ann Arbor on a Saturday afternoon in the autumn, there are but a few rural Wolverine fans. The vast majority of rural folks are wearing green and rooting for the Spartans of Michigan State up in East Lansing. Okay, I might live on a northern Illinois farm and be a Bear fan along with my urban Chicago brother, but that's not much of a connection to bind society.

The majority of Americans are now urban/suburban and are increasingly clustered on the two coasts and in northern Illinois. Yet the great majority of land surface remains rural. The two are deeply divided. And both groups have large majorities that are living unhappy lives. Toss into this mix the behavior of the elites in America which Murray describes as unseemly and increasingly tied to knowing the right federal official, and we are left with "hollowness at the core."[27] Not a pretty picture.

The Destructive National Discourse

The enormous and constantly growing cultural chasm in our country is highly significant due to two other factors present in our society. First, we are obtaining information from an increasingly concentrated national media that is also increasingly pervasive in our daily lives. This media is populated by urban elitists, which is nothing new in our culture. What is relatively new is their power to influence national discussion and national will. Second, the importance of this media influence derives from the incessant growth of the national Central Authority we call the federal government. This state of affairs gives the "10 percenters" enormous power if they are on the side of the urban media elite. The urban elite influence not just New York politics but national policy. And national policy now affects every aspect of human life, including life of the yet unborn, in every corner of the land.

The media elite remains far, far away from much of America. Andrew Ross Sorkin, a young favorite of the New York elite who is a financial columnist for the *New York Times* and co-anchors Squawk Box on CNBC, thought that hot dogs in convenience stores sat on the grill all day with no one eating them. He wondered if they keep them all week or rotate them into the trash. There was a general discussion among the three anchor persons and bets over how many might actually be consumed. The tenor of the conversation was in the vein of, "Who in their right mind would eat one of these?" He was informed later that several million are sold every day. He had no idea of how millions of Americans who work out of big rigs, pickups, and delivery vans catch a meal. Nor is there any reason he should have known. His limousine driver ferries him from Manhattan to the studio in New Jersey and back. He does not own a car. In another Squawk Box discussion, anchor Becky Quick wondered where in the US do we grow sugar and how is it processed. My reaction to both of these discussions was "Omigosh!"

Large swaths of American life listen to or watch national media and shake their heads over the ignorance of powerful people advocating national behavior norms. As a result, people are migrating to news sources that are compatible with their view of life, behavior, and government. This growing splinter of media influence is perhaps helpful in stemming the power of the 10 percenters since they may be talking more and more to each other. But that condition leads to even more stridency in the discourse of like-minded citizens and further aggravates the divide. In addition, the blogs and unedited writings asserting unverifiable facts now abound across the Internet. Hundreds of these brief essays are published daily and circulate nationally, most of which are destructive of any notion of unity.

Propelling this destructive discourse is the reality that people make a lot of money and corporations generate enormous wealth pandering to our wants and fears. The federal government stands ready to expand its power in any fashion deemed popular. The media creates popularity. Those in favor of an issue are watching, and those against an issue dare not ignore the debate lest defeat occur for lack of advocacy. An issue can be raised by anyone having access to the media elite. And the media elite is hungrily seeking potential drama to lure listeners and watchers to its programming and advertising.

The Destructive Clutter of Divisive Issues

In this environment of advocacy in favor of or in fear of increasing Central Authority, fomented daily by a media bent on maximizing profit, we have beset ourselves with numerous highly divisive issues of human behavior that are devouring our national discourse. None of these issues are capable of national resolution, and all of them highlight the growing chasm of culture. All of them should be red herrings in the debate over the future of America. But each of them is highly significant and potentially the canary in the coal mine only because the Central Authority would make one rule for all.

Immigration

Immigration policy is only a divisive issue because of the national welfare state. We need immigrants to come here as guest workers to do seasonal work others don't want to do. Immigrants learn that if they stay here without work, or even with part-time work, they can obtain IDs to access the welfare state and public education for their children. Life is better than where they came from. So they stay, work for cash, and add to our welfare cost. Before the welfare state, immigrants could come here if they had a job and a sponsor. No one would come here to starve. People came to work and stayed working or went home. We don't have an immigration problem; we have a welfare state problem. There are several complicated issues with respect to immigration, but we could address these issues forthrightly. Yet we choose not to do so, making the matter utterly divisive.

Marriage

Marriage is a religious rite among Jews and Christians, as well as among other religious peoples, creating a bond between a man and a woman that our society recognized and honored to varying degrees over our history by allocating property, care of children, and economic support in the event of death of a spouse or dissolution. Society also made rules regarding the man, woman, and children as a family unit, allocating health care, social security benefits, and the like among members of the unit. The married state now confers societal economic benefits. It's all about the money.

Homosexual relationships have never been acknowledged in the history of the Jews or the Christians under the rite of marriage, but we now are engaged in a fierce debate over the right of homosexuals to be married. This debate is utterly unnecessary and disastrously divisive. States wishing to celebrate the homosexual relationship and raise its status to that enjoyed by married couples and family units should simply create a civil union status with such rights. Those not wishing to do so should refrain.

Homosexuals will gravitate to those regions that celebrate their lifestyle. Devout Christians and Jews will gravitate to those regions that honor their lifestyle. Why do we insist on a national rule that punches Christians and Jews in their collective nose or tries to insist homosexuals can't form a civil union? The issue is only significant and therefore divisive because money flows from the Central Authority in consequence.

The best solution to this problem on a national scale is to simply eliminate all rights to money for spouses. Then the word *marriage* can remain defined as a union between a man and a woman among those religious peoples who wish to define the rite as such.

Guns

Gun ownership is a right under the Constitution and a flashpoint in the great majority of land mass in the country. Hunting and personal security are important to life in rural America. The county sheriff or state trooper may be an hour away from an urgent need for help. In urban areas, the societal needs may warrant the registration and control of firearms by authorities. This issue should be local, not national. Local laws are not a threat to freedom. Like-minded citizens should be able to proscribe gun use and security. Those who are not of the community's mind can gravitate to a locale outside the jurisdiction if the matter is that important to them. The issue becomes divisive and destructive only when the 10 percenters want to make a rule for everyone across this great land.

The Unborn

The sanctity of life is to Christians a matter not subject to the debate of relativity. Life is a gift of God that is not to be tampered with, either in the womb or as we approach the end of our days. Abortion and suicide are not condoned. A society that does so is not a society that Christians can fully embrace. A decree by the Supreme Court that there is somehow a constitutional right to abortion was wholly wrong and has perpetuated a fractious and utterly divisive debate. Let it be. Our society will not judge a woman for terminating her pregnancy. Leave it alone. If it is not the society you like very much, then let God be the judge. Christians should be able to live their lives as they define Christian behavior and let the nonbelievers or Christian compromisers do as they will. Making one rule for all either way is a disaster.

If you want to get an abortion, a morning-after remedy, or commit suicide, don't expect a Catholic hospital or other Christian religious institution to accommodate your wish. Go elsewhere. It's your problem created by your own behavior. Not theirs. On the other side of things, states that make laws proscribing the behavior invite turmoil in their attempt to convert nonbelievers by secular action. It is hard to see how such action leads to peace and harmony.

As a people, we need to focus more on the real issue rather than the human right. An abortion or a suicide or a homicide is at root a human failure and a human tragedy. These human actions are a cause for sadness, not societal anger. Our society is not sustaining itself. White European origin births are at the rate of 1.6. Blacks are even less. Neither will sustain either race. The much higher birthrate among Hispanics and Muslims raise the overall American level to 2.1, barely a sustainable rate for our society as a whole. The real issue for our society is our lack of interest in birthing and raising children to carry on when we are gone. As with much of our debate, we miss the human reality exposed by our selfish desires.

Special Preferences

The special preferences our Central Authority awards to classes of people is not so destructively divisive as it is a constant reminder of how the political class corrupts our society with perpetual victimization to maintain its power. The affirmative action social idea of fifty years ago has long lost its moral credibility, as has the governmental bias for gender equality. We have moved from a nation striving for equal opportunity to one of equality in result. To achieve the latter, our Central Authority has created a labyrinth of special preferences for minority classes, both perceived and actual, such that all the preferred classes now comprise a majority voting bloc for preservation of these preferences.

One typically absurd example of preferences is the USDA's decision in September 2012 just before the presidential election to offer $1.3 billion to women and Hispanics who were denied subsidized farm loans or said that they did not apply for such loans but would have liked to have done so between 1981 and 2000. This attempt to correct past perceived discrimination follows the past practice of awarding billions of dollars to blacks who claimed to be victims of USDA discrimination (nothing more required) during the period 1981-1996. Over ninety thousand claims were filed before the 2012 deadline, although the Census Bureau estimates that there were no more than thirty-three thousand farms nationwide operated by blacks during the period.

The corruptive influence of special preference awards in contracts, subsidies, jobs, and educational opportunity have come to far outweigh the perceived social benefits. The Central Authority is simply buying votes to maintain its power, and it is taxing those it does not favor by limiting their opportunity to participate in a competitive marketplace. This practice, when pervasive, undermines the consent of the governed.

All Together Now

With the specter of impoverishment from a decline in our empire, our unfunded promises to those in need and facing retirement, our printing of money and fear of confiscatory taxation, we have set up the public classes against the private classes and the have-nots against the haves in a zero-sum no-growth clash of classes. This coming clash is sorting itself out roughly between urban and rural, but more so within particular states and state governments, while the national media encourages in nasty discourse to debate the divisions rather than acknowledge accommodation.

Political Division

The political map demonstrates that our division as a people has shifted from where we came from or how we make a living to where we live. Our division is now increasingly geographic which augers greatly for serious trouble ahead. Not since the 1850s have we seen such a stark geographical political divide.

In part, the division is the traditional urban/rural split. Virginia is a good example. The map below shows that of the eleven congressional districts, two are Democrat and nine are Republican. The Republicans have a majority of the legislature. But the state was carried by the Democrat in the presidential tally due to the heavy urban/suburban vote near Washington, DC, and along the coastal rivers. Over 90 percent of the land mass is occupied by red state citizens who are outnumbered by their urban blue staters concentrated near centers of power.

Virginia's Presidential Vote in 2012

Republican Candidate	Democrat Candidate
(white area)	(dark area)

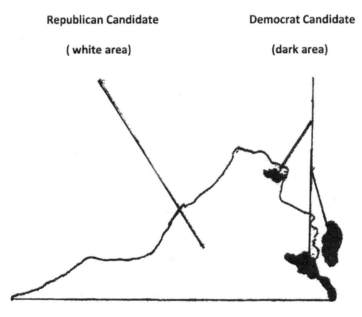

Source: *The Economist*, February 9, 2013, 31

However, the divide is not simply the historic rural/urban because in a large swath of the country, those living in cities increasingly have tended to vote similar patterns to those living in rural areas. The map below shows voting preferences in the 2012 presidential election by state. In twenty-three red states (shown white), the preference was for the Republican candidate, and in twenty-seven blue states (shown dark), the preference was for the Democrat candidate. The red states account for approximately 36 percent of the nation's population and 64 percent of our land mass.

2012 Presidential Election

Republican Red States   Democrat Blue States

(Shown White)   (Shown Dark)

Source: *The Economist*, February 9, 2013, 31

If one were to extend the presidential election map to voting preferences by county, the figure below shows that the eastern 60 percent of California, Oregon, and Washington, nearly all of Nevada, the northern 60 percent of Florida, the western 60 percent of Pennsylvania, 90 percent of Virginia, and the southern 60 percent of Ohio and Illinois would attach to the red state preferences, occupying about 76 percent of the United States land area.

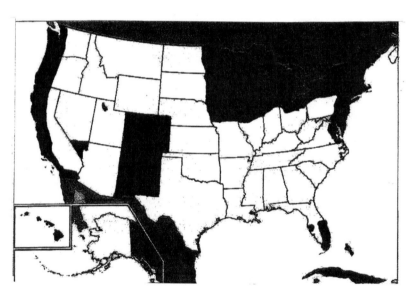

Source: *The Wall Street Journal,* November 8, 2012

Republicans now control a majority of state legislatures, including the blue presidential election states of Wisconsin, Michigan, Ohio, Pennsylvania, and

Florida. Increasingly, one political party so dominates a state that legislative control can override a governor's veto. Fully half the state legislatures have veto-proof one-party control in 2013, of which nine are Democrat and sixteen are Republican. There is something very significant going on here that is relevant to the subject matter of this book. We are not merely lining up as individuals on one side or the other of the many social and economic issues. We are now expressing ourselves in voting blocs to control county and state governments characterized by these differing values. In short, we are getting organized to prevail in our separate Ways of Life.

No Peace in Our Time

The prevailing notion that we can just continue to muddle through and get along while we sort out our differences is no longer rational. Our national debt is crushing us, and our excess annual spending requires even more borrowing. Our current Way of Life as defined and mandated by the Central Authority is unsustainable.

We cannot remain a united people who are simply divided on the issue of government as ruler, protector, and provider mandating one Way of Life any more than we could remain a united people who were simply divided on the issue of slavery. Just as the institution of slavery was neither static nor contained geographically, today our monstrous Central Authority is growing steadily and independently both in reach and in intensity of control.

These institutions, most notably the so-called independent federal bureaucracies, will not leave us alone and, when threatened, will take extraordinary measures to strike fear in the populace, subvert rules to thwart public debate, distort their mandates, ignore both the Congress and federal judiciary, and intimidate with threatened fines and other actions to force compliance or face the risk of large legal fees to defend one's freedom.

The appetite of the Central Authority for ever more power is insatiable. We are fast approaching that moment in time when elections seem not to matter much in 70 percent of our land mass. We have already passed the tipping point as we shall discuss in the next chapter. What remains is some as yet undefinable federal action or series of actions that will cause a significant portion of the population to separate itself from the Union. Then we will know we have had our Last Election.

In the end, we must agree on a Way of Life that is sustainable, or our entire society will collapse into an unstable series of regions and communities bent first on survival and then on stability and growth. Before the collapse, will we find some other more orderly path to agreement on separate Ways of Life, permitting us to abide peaceably on this continent?

Two Ways of Life

Then and Now

America in the 1850s and 2010s

Incompatible Ways of Life

As a free people organized to govern ourselves, we have had since 1776 the obligation to determine our own Way of Life. We rejected the notion that a king should define our way of living. We would do this ourselves. We set out to protect ourselves, knowing full well that the great weight of human history has the common theme of man's attempt to bring other men into bondage. Humans formed communities to protect themselves from other communities who would seek to dominate them. But then we also needed to be mindful of protecting ourselves within our own community from others who would bind and exploit us to their will. Our Constitution and Bill of Rights addressed both the former and the latter. In ratifying these documents, we agreed on a social regimen here in this nation that would be our common Way of Life.

In doing so, however, we made a big mistake, not knowing at the time that this mistake was so big that it would come to tear our nation in two with enormous loss of life in a bloody Civil War. In forming our common Way of Life, we acknowledged as a nation of white people that black people were so inferior as to be relegated to the status of common property to be owned and dealt with by white people as one would deal with a common farm implement. Black Africans did not immigrate independently to these shores. These poor humans were captured in Africa and hauled here as human property relegated to a life of slavery to white masters.

Human slavery had been a historical fact throughout recorded human history. As a reality in human existence, it simply was there. When we formed our Republic, we acknowledged it much as we acknowledged other human activity that more or fewer of us did not countenance. We did not let it prevent our forming a union. We would abide together for more significant goals and not let our disagreements regarding this social regimen divide us.

Over time the division grew as citizens in northern states, for numerous reasons relating to climate, the nature of industrial labor, religious values, and cultural heritage, among others, eliminated the practice of owning black people as slaves. In the southern states, slave labor provided the economic underpinning of a prosperous agricultural society and grew significantly in the late eighteenth and early nineteenth centuries. The import of slaves from Africa ceased as a legal activity in 1808, but the slave-based society in the South became evermore entrenched. Essentially, as a nation we grew to adopt not one common Way of Life, but two very different Ways of Life.

These two Ways of Life were utterly incompatible from the beginning, but we either didn't know it or didn't wish to confront it. How we chose to deal with this incompatibility over a half century is instructive for us today as we experience a growing awareness of two incompatible Ways of Life hurtling into tomorrow on a collision course.

Today our two incompatible Ways of Life may be described essentially as on the one hand a Way of Life in which control of nearly all human behavior is held by a central power and its agency bureaus and on the other hand a Way of Life that minimizes central authority, leaving human behavior largely in the hands of the individual, small communities, and states. Although the incompatible social regimens today and those of the first half of the nineteenth century are different in material respects, the parallels are starkly sobering and profoundly real. The struggle has the age-old common theme of human history—human bondage. Consider the period 1850 to 1860 in relation to our nation today. And consider the similarity of events, then and now.

Then

The Prelude: 1789-1850

Until the 1850s the vast majority of citizens in the northern states ignored the matter of slavery in the

South. The regimen had been eliminated in their states. There was no love for the black race, nor any notion of human equality. Blacks and slavery were not their problem. Northern whites had problems of their own to solve, clearing the wilderness, dealing with the native Indian populations, building roads, bridges, railroads, canals, ports, and steamships to carry immigrants into the lands bordering the Great Lakes. The Constitution acknowledged two separate social societies, and that was that.

During this period, enormous wealth was developing in the slave states east of the Mississippi. This wealth produced economic and political power. Southern lore counts more millionaires in Natchez along the Mississippi in 1850 than in New York City. An Alabama senator estimated that slave property in 1850 was worth over $900 million,[28] equating to over $50 billion today. The financial elite along the East Coast benefited greatly by economic exploitation of the slave property, including the cotton trade exported from the South and the numerous imports bought with the proceeds. The wealthy elite along the East Coast and in the South were content with the status quo.

Enslavement of black Africans created a vibrant economy, placed enormous wealth in the hands of a few, put America on the global trade map, and benefited everyone. Jefferson Davis, the Mississippi cotton baron who would later lead the Confederacy, maintained that, "Human bondage . . . was fully justified by the Bible, validated by the U.S. Constitution, and a blessing for the slaves themselves, since they had been delivered from human 'sacrifice' by the barbarians of their African homeland."[29] An ethic developed among the Southern elite to justify the slavery regimen. And a companion ethic developed among the Northeastern elite to accommodate the South. This accommodation was good for business and preserved the Union.

The principal challenge in maintaining this accommodation of two Ways of Life was political, involving the Congress and the elites. By 1820 they had to figure out how to expand our national governance west of the Mississippi River. Territories and states would be organized in the lands of the Louisiana Purchase. Maine had applied for statehood as a free state, which would have upset the even balance of power in the Senate. When Missouri applied for statehood, the South insisted that it be permitted to choose for itself. Missouri joined the Union in 1821 and chose to permit slave ownership, keeping the delicate power balance.

However, the growing aversion in the North to slavery as a social regimen, together with the passion in the South over maintaining its Way of Life and the ability to expand it, brought about a fierce debate in Congress over which social regimen would prevail in the territories. Missouri's statehood application was held hostage to this debate. They ended up drawing a line on the southern border of Missouri. Below that line, one could own slaves, and above that line, except for Missouri, slaveholding would be prohibited.

In the Missouri Compromise of 1820, slavery was now permitted to expand past the Mississippi into the Louisiana Purchase to the West. The Compromise to preserve the Union and settle the matter was woefully short of vision, perhaps because vision was not the matter at hand. At hand was compromise to keep the Union together for that time. Also at hand was the sudden realization that the slavery regimen threatened to erupt in civil war. The South learned in the debates of 1820 that the balance of power in the House was lost to the growing Northern population, notwithstanding the boost in counting 60 percent of slaves as citizens for apportionment. The North learned that the South would fight, even if it came to blood, to preserve its Way of Life. "Slaveholders had also learned something else that would prove to be of great political value: that enough Northerners were sufficiently frightened of the nation's collapse that they could be bullied into surrendering their principles when it came to slavery."[30]

From 1820 to 1850 the political compromise held. During this period, life was good for white landowners in the South. Louisiana, Arkansas, and Texas promised room for growth of slave agriculture. Balance in the Senate and bullying the Northeastern elite fearful of a potential financial collapse promised continued prosperity for the Southern Way of Life. Yet underneath the veneer of this young nation, there was growing disgust with the social regimen of slavery. Runaway slaves to the North and into Canada were aided in ever-increasing numbers by fellow citizens north of the Ohio River and the Pennsylvania border. Black Africans settled in Northern communities and became a meaningful part of the social fabric, attending church, assisting fellow citizens, and acting as good neighbors. Southern slave owners traveling north to reclaim their property were not welcome and found less and less assistance in their efforts. Underneath the veneer, the social fabric was slowly coming unglued. The two Ways of Life were growing incompatible.

By 1850, the nation was seriously divided. We remained together only because no event forced us into conflict. Then two very significant events occurred nearly simultaneously. In 1849, gold was discovered in California, and by 1850, the territory was ungovernable. It had to establish a government either as a state or its own nation. The pressure on Washington to admit California as a state was overwhelming. However, California would not countenance slavery. It would be a free state or no state at all. And half or more of California, north to the Big Sur and Monterey area, lay south of the Missouri Compromise latitude line of 36 degrees, 30 minutes.

The second significant event was the victory in the Mexican War and the Treaty of Guadalupe Hidalgo executed in July 1848, which ceded to the United States all the lands north of the Rio Grande and west to include what is now New Mexico, Arizona, Southern California, and portions of Utah, Colorado, and Wyoming. Complicating matters was the fact that the western border of Texas had never been defined because it included land claimed by Mexico. Now that land was part of the United States. Texas wanted for its state everything west to the north/south run of the Rio Grande, which included Albuquerque and Santa Fe, half of today's New Mexico. The Spanish population of this area along the Rio Grande did not want slavery. New Mexico would never come into the nation as a slave state when the time came for statehood. Texas was a slave state. By 1850, Texas had decided to assert itself and sent its own forces to seize Santa Fe. The US Army was dispatched to assert control of the territory. Civil war was at hand. All this land that would eventually become New Mexico and Arizona lay below the Missouri Compromise line. In 1850, the United States government had to act on California, the Mexican territories, and Texas. Yet the nation was seriously and emotionally divided.

The Run-up: 1850-1860

A House Divided

The Congress was politically divided, reflecting the nation's division on a number of issues. There were two principal political parties, neither of which was organized in favor of or in opposition to the slavery regimen. The Democrats favored a more agrarian society, states' rights, and a small federal authority, while the Whigs favored a more robust national effort to promote industry and growth. Both parties had members in the North and South. And neither party was prepared to deal with the events in 1850. An opening foray into the matter occurred in 1846 as America went to war with Mexico, when David Wilmot, an obscure Pennsylvania Democrat, introduced a bill in the House of Representatives. The so-called Wilmot Proviso would prevent slavery from being introduced in any territory acquired in the war, a complete abrogation of the Missouri Compromise of 1820.

Complicating matters further was a new antislavery party created in 1848, called the Free Soil Party, dominated by former Whig members. In the House of Representatives, the Whigs held a small majority at the end of the previous Congress, but at the beginning of the new session, they could not elect a Speaker without the Free Soilers, most of whom voted as a block for their own man. The tiny Free Soil Party of nine men scattered among six northern states held the balance of power in the House. Over the course of nearly three weeks, the House conducted sixty-two ballots with no majority before resolving to elect a Speaker by a mere plurality on the sixty-third. During the balloting, there had been clandestine deal making with the Free Soilers which, upon discovery, threw the House into chaos, replete with fiery accusations, threats of secession and war, and a melee of members which included the gallery. Historian Fergus Bordewich's well-documented account reads like a dime novel.[31] For the first time in our history, the fate of the slavery regimen was now out in the open and on the table. Democrat Howell Cobb, a Georgian and wealthy plantation owner, was elected Speaker.

Bordewich concludes, "The slaveholding South had once again prevailed. And the anti-slavery movement had shown that it had the power to cripple moderate Whigs, in a foretaste of countless political contests that would take place in the northern states in the years to come."[32] A tiny fraction of single-issue true believers in the righteousness of their cause, representing only 4 percent of the House, the Free Soilers succeeded in exposing the fault lines of a hopelessly divided nation, ultimately crippling the détente that accommodated the slavery regimen and Southern Way of Life.

A Grand Bargain that Failed

Those sober leaders who would preserve the Union knew that a grand bargain, a great compromise of all pressing issues on the slavery regimen, must be made to settle the nation and assure its future promise. A great lion of the Senate, Henry Clay of Kentucky, nearing the end of his career and his life, proposed a grand compromise. He enlisted the support of Daniel Webster, fellow Whig from New York, and offered something for every constituency. His plan had the following elements: (1) California be admitted to statehood with permission to decide on its own the matter of slavery; (2) creation of the New Mexico and Arizona territories with no mention of slavery; (3) formation of the western Texan boundary with a line running east northeast from El Paso to the Red River, which eliminated most of New Mexico and the current panhandle, but pay off Texas's public debt in compensation; (4) maintain slavery in the District of Columbia but ban slave trading there; and (5) a tough fugitive slave law requiring return of human slave property and restitution for damage together with a federal ban on interference with slave trade among slaveholding states.[33] Preserve the Southern Way of Life, prevent its expansion, protect the property of slaveholders, and mollify Texas. A grand bargain indeed.

Clay's effort to pass these compromise resolutions failed as no majority constituency could be found for the whole plan among thirty-six Democrats, twenty-four Whigs, and two Free Soilers in the Senate. In April, a special committee of six northerners and six southerners was formed with Clay as the chairman. The Committee of Thirteen, as it was called, worked to thrash out agreement on all of Clay's proposals and group them into an omnibus bill. The bill was introduced and hotly debated. Filibusters raged. The omnibus ultimately failed. The division over slavery, once out in the open, not only transcended party lines and loyalties but was so intense that each issue in the debate was virtually nonnegotiable.

Stop Gap Measures

Fortunately, for the temporary preservation of the Union, Stephen Douglas, the young senator from Illinois, figured out that while there was no majority for Clay's grand bargain, there were majorities to be had from different factions on each of the plan's elements. He also had the advantage of a Senate grown exhausted with debate and miserably hot in Washington's late summer. The Texas boundary was set where it is today supported by moderates in the north and south. Firebrand Free Soilers and rabid slaveholders were in the minority. California was the big deal. Admitting California as a free state would destroy the North/ South balance in the Senate. Slave states would be in the minority. Sam Houston of Texas broke the deadlock with support, acknowledging the effect, but hoping the discord would end, and championing the Union. After that, there was little fight on the new territories. The tough new fugitive slave law demanded by the South was passed with fifteen Northern senators, including the young Mr. Douglas, abstaining or otherwise avoiding the votes. Why? Perhaps because they would just as soon not have to deal with the runaway slave issue but did not want to be seen by their constituents voting for the law.[34]

The House acted quickly, with the seasoned Mr. Cobb in charge and the energetic Stephen Douglas lobbying strenuously from his Senate post. Again, it was the politics of dividing up the measures to cobble together a majority. The most raucous debate was over the territories of New Mexico and what is now Arizona below the Missouri line. Texas, having been bought off with a border compromise and money, helped with winning the majority on the territories. The Deep South was enraged. The tough Fugitive Slave Law passed, again without much debate. Northerners intent on mollifying the South found themselves conveniently absent for the vote. The Senate approved the work of the House and the Grand Compromise was signed into law by President Fillmore, though it is said that he agonized over the Fugitive Slave Law for two days. Everyone patted themselves on the back. The Union had been preserved. California was in. The territories had governments. Texas had a firm border. On the surface there was calm.

A Bad Law Makes Matters Worse

The 1850 Compromise soon proved to be an empty vessel. The Kansas-Nebraska Act of 1854 resulted from the pressing need to establish territorial governments west of the Mississippi in the Great Plains so that citizens could establish homestead property rights to land they would settle and farm.

All this territory was north of the Missouri Compromise line, supposedly to be free of slavery, and the South was in no mood to permit territory status to this vast tract of land that included current-day Kansas, Nebraska, the Dakotas, and parts of Colorado, Wyoming, and Montana. To accommodate the South, Stephen Douglas, again the political artist, proposed establishing both a Kansas and a Nebraska territory and successfully argued that the Compromise of 1850 nullified the Missouri Compromise, leaving territories to decide for themselves whether or not to permit slaveholding.

The South was determined to make Kansas a slaveholding territory, while the abolitionists of the North were determined to prevent slavery north of the Missouri Compromise line. What ensued was a bloodbath in Kansas waged between the two groups, often with the assistance of armed thugs.

The low-level civil war waged in the territory, known as Bleeding Kansas, over the one issue of slavery was a harbinger of things to come. The Jayhawker abolitionist immigrants eventually won the demographic contest, and Kansas entered the Union as a free state in 1861.

The Division Intensifies

Underneath, the South seethed with anger and fretted with angst. They were now a minority people subjugated to the will of a growing Northern majority seemingly unbound by precedent, the Constitution, or the law. In the ensuing decade, secession talk grew. Conventions were held. And the Fugitive Slave Law was actively enforced. The law imposed a heavy fine on anyone who interfered with recapture or otherwise abetted the runaway slave, thus significantly improving the ability of Southern slaveholders to retrieve their property.

In the North, the abolitionists morphed from the status of dangerous crackpots in 1850 to that of mainstream morality as more and more white citizens experienced the wrenching capture and enslavement of black men, women, and children in their communities. A law that was intended to protect the property of slave owners in the South did so at the cost of slowly bringing the North to stark awareness of the cruelty and inhumanity of the slavery regimen. But perhaps more than any other factor, the turmoil disturbed the peace in Northern communities. The Southern Way of Life became a bothersome nuisance in the North such that the people there could not live free of its presence in their midst.

The abolition movement led to the disintegration of the Whig Party and the creation of the Republican Party in 1854, a development utterly unforeseeable in 1850 four years previous. The tiny Free Soilers of the 1850 debates now were leaders in a new national party that nominated a presidential candidate in 1856 and elected a president in 1860.

The Supreme Court Is No Help

With the Congress hopelessly divided, there was some hope that the Supreme Court would settle matters to create some finality or pathway to finality on the matter of slavery. No such luck. A major event of the decade was the Dred Scott decision by the Supreme Court in 1857. The court's ruling held that the Missouri Compromise was unconstitutional in that the federal government had no right to interfere with the property rights of its citizens. Slaves were property, not citizens. Hence, they could be taken by their owners in any part of the nation and territories as the property of their owners, regardless of whether a particular state or territory permitted the ownership of slaves. The case arose because Mr. Scott had been taken by his master into two free states and then back to a slave state. He sued for his freedom, arguing that by taking him into a free state, he then became a free man.

The Supreme Court's decision has been condemned broadly for its inhumane and utterly barbarian attitude toward the black race. Politically, the court stunned the North by abrogating all laws regarding the abolition of slavery. At the time of the decision, five of the justices were from the South (Maryland, Virginia, Tennessee, Georgia, and Alabama) and four from the North (Ohio, New York, Pennsylvania, and Massachusetts). Given the politics of the era, this split would not be unusual.

In the seven to two majority, the five Southern justices voted with the majority along with two Northerners.

The sweeping thirty-nine-page opinion made clear that under a strict construction of the Constitution, no other conclusion could be reached. Chief Justice Taney, a Maryland lawyer and quite possibly the owner of slaves, together with his majority, were not unmindful of the politics of the day or of the political impact of their ruling. The opinion, read in its entirety, is more a history lesson than an arcane legal analysis.[35] Taney was matter of fact but clearly uncomfortable.

On strict construction:

It is not the province of the court to decide upon the justice or injustice, the policy or impolicy, of these laws. The decision of that question belonged to the political or lawmaking power, to those who formed the sovereignty and framed the Constitution. The duty of the court is to interpret the instrument they have framed with the best lights we can obtain on the subject, and to administer it as we find it, according to its true intent and meaning when it was adopted.[36]

On matter of fact:

It is difficult at this day to realize the state of public opinion in relation to that unfortunate race which prevailed in the civilized and enlightened portions of the world at the time of the Declaration of Independence and when the Constitution of the United States was framed and adopted. But the public history of every European nation displays it in a manner too plain to be mistaken.[37]

Justice Taney then proceeds to lay out the behavior and attitude of the white race toward the black race in England and the colonies. He calls out in particular the behavior of Northern colonial and state legislative actions. The entire opinion is a classic reading out of racism in America.

The Supreme Court, when confronted with the issue head on in Dred Scott, made a mockery of all the so-called compromises in the Congress. The case is cited for many things it is not. It should be cited perhaps, first, as a concise rendition of white racism in its ugliest reality by a sober court and, second, as a landmark example of the court reminding Congress and the people that they adopted a Constitution to restrain the unbridled majority from making things up as they see fit at any one time.

When the people cannot bring themselves to change the Constitution, the court cannot do that for them and should not make the attempt. If the people cannot come to a decision peaceably through amendment to their Constitution, then they invite civil war. The court cannot do one or prevent the other. That is the meaning of Dred Scott.

The Absence of Leadership

From 1820 to 1850, the nation reconciled itself to its division into two separate yet politically equal Ways of Life. From 1850 to 1860, the nation grew to realize that these two Ways of Life were not only incompatible but would one day result in a breakup of the nation into separate countries or the destruction of one or the other Way of Life. It is perhaps not surprising, but worth noting, that during this time the nation elected as its president remarkably ineffective men. Few Americans today could name any of the presidents in the twenty years leading up to the Civil War: Harrison, Tyler, Polk, Taylor, Fillmore, Pierce, and Buchanan. Two died in office shortly after election. Four were Whigs, and three were Democrats.

In the early 1850s, the great orators of the Senate left the chamber, most through death. Clay, Webster, and Calhoun, to name three, were gone. No one took their place save the political operator, Stephen Douglas, of Illinois who gave us Bleeding Kansas. And the Supreme Court in Dred Scott cursed the whole lot for creating this mess. A pox on you all. No presidential leadership. No congressional leadership. And no court to bail everyone out with a Solomon-like decree. One might ask, Is it any wonder that we slipped into chaos?

Inevitable Conflict

There is something about the human condition that augers for one man to prevail over another, one Way of Life to prevail over another. Perhaps we are driven by fear as much as by lust. The Southern Way of Life sought expansion to protect its very existence as much as in lust for more wealth and power.

The Northern Way of Life sought to contain and suppress the Southern Way of Life as much for fear of losing competitive advantage as its distaste for the slavery regimen in human behavior. Both societies feared and distrusted one another, not just as political adversaries but as threats to their very Way of Life.

When leadership finally did present itself in the form of Abraham Lincoln, the die was cast. The nation as a whole clearly did not want strong leadership on this issue. Strong leadership meant confrontation. And confrontation meant war, not reconciliation, as the outcome. The reason was simple. The nature of the debate on the nation's divide changed. Lincoln changed it.

In his debates with Stephen Douglas in late summer 1858 for the Senate, Lincoln transformed the slavery regimen from a political issue to a moral question. While he assured his audiences that he as a white man would advocate the continued superiority of the white race over the black race, he argued that slavery was wrong. In the course of the debates, Lincoln grew in his own conviction as he wrestled verbally and intellectually with his able adversary. By the end of the debates, he must have realized that he could not straddle the fence. Regardless of public sentiment in southern Illinois, where the debates occurred, favoring public sovereignty in the territories and new states to determine the slavery question for themselves, Lincoln finally took the stand that slavery must not be allowed to grow because it is morally wrong. At the final debate in Alton, Lincoln addressed the matter, now clear in his mind,

> It is the same spirit that says, "You work and toil and earn bread, and I'll eat it." No matter in what shape it comes, whether from the mouth of a king who seeks to bestride the people of his own nation and live by the fruit of their labor, or from one race of men as an apology for enslaving another race, it is the same tyrannical principle.[38]

Lincoln lost the race for the Senate in Illinois but enhanced the stature of the young Republican Party, such that as its presidential candidate in 1860, he defeated Democrat Stephen Douglas and two southern candidates, winning a majority of the Electoral College votes while gaining only about 40 percent of the popular vote. The North now had 60 percent of the Electoral College votes due to its much larger population, and Lincoln won them all. Douglas ran as a Northern Democrat and won only Missouri, which was a slave state. The southern states voted for the southern Democrat, Breckenridge, and the Constitutional Union candidate, Bell from Tennessee.

It would be our Last Election. No one could look at the results and conclude otherwise. We had become a single-issue nation. The issue was slavery and the Southern Way of Life. There were more people in the North, more electoral votes under our Constitution, and they would have their way notwithstanding Chief Justice Taney and a large majority of the Supreme

Court that ruled the Constitution forbid any such action by the federal government. The Southern Way of Life would not be allowed to expand. The rule of the majority would be used to repress, contain, and in every way possible extinguish that which the majority vehemently disfavored. How could the Southerners be ruled by a government that considered their Way of Life to be morally wrong? How long would the Northern Way of Life permit the existence of the morally wrong Southern Way? How could one be secure in his Way of Life and in his community? The time for separation had come.

Now

The Prelude: 1935-2005

As we discussed in chapter 1, the beginning of the march back into human bondage began during Franklin Roosevelt's first term in the 1930s with the establishment of independent federal regulatory agencies under broad legislation that is capable of bureaucratic interpretation without further congressional lawmaking. At its heart, it is an elitist notion; namely, that the sophisticated New York brain trust can and should do for Americans what they are too stupid or ignorant to do for themselves. Over the ensuing seventy years, these federal agencies, and several more that were created during the period, have come to control nearly every aspect of human activity from a Central Authority in Washington directed by the executive branch.

The growth of these federal institutions was met from time to time with resistance, but the process was so gradual, and always justified by noble social progress aspirations, that we have come to accept them as a necessary part of the American fabric. We knew that Congress could control them by enacting new laws and conducting oversight hearings. So in a representative form of government, these institutions would certainly reflect the majority will of the people.

As an example, the Food and Drug Administration protects our food supply and restricts the sale of drugs until proved effective by scientific study. We know that elitists are continually influencing the FDA to ban or restrict foods and drugs to foster their own ideas of the ideal Way of Life. And yes, some people die for lack of experimental drugs not permitted by FDA. Some businesses are destroyed and jobs lost by regulations based on faulty science. But we abide because most of us are not affected adversely to our knowledge, and most of us think that we do benefit from FDA. The same comment could be made about most regulatory agencies over the period 1935 through 1965. They must be serving their purpose or Congress would step in to change the laws. And most important, their work really does not affect me personally.

In 1965, with the passage of the Great Society legislation and the ensuing decade, there was a major increase in regulatory authority. So much so that even *Time* magazine in the late 1970s had a cover with Health, Education and Welfare Secretary Joe Califano hopelessly encircled in red tape. The nation fell into a *malaise*, the term acknowledged by our then president. A new word, *stagflation*, was coined for high inflation and no growth. The welfare state brought on by the

Great Society legislation was creating large permanent deficits. And we were still incurring the expense of the Cold War. Millions of blue-collar union workers and their families realized finally that they were the ones paying the bill because there were more of them than anyone else.

In 1980, the Reagan Democrats elected a Republican president and a Republican Senate. Major tax reform ensued, and the growth of the Federal Register of new regulations declined . . . but the federal government continued to grow. And federal deficit spending also continued. In 1980, the federal debt was about $900 billion. In the next eight years, the debt grew over 200 percent to $2.6 trillion, nearly 50 percent of gross national product. A brief reverie followed the collapse of the Soviet Union and the Berlin Wall in the late 1980s, but Americans were finally realizing that they had created a monster of a federal government with uncontrollable entitlements to all manner of constituencies and independent bureaucratic agencies bent on constant expansion of their spheres of influence. If tax rates were to remain moderate enough to permit savings and economic growth, the federal government and its constant burden of increasing regulatory costs could not be sustained.

Since the mid-1980s, we have realized that we simply don't know how to contain what we have created. We have tried all manner of politics, from divided government to one-party rule, trying first the Republicans, then switching to the Democrats, then back to the Republicans. We have embraced to some degree third-party candidates with a clear message, enough so that a Democrat president was elected without a majority in 1992. None of our efforts to find the right leader or the right political party or mix or parties has been effective. The national debt and national regulation continued to grow.

It is difficult to know when we passed the tipping point, but we have certainly done so. The evidence is that political power is now such an enormous economic prize that it corrupts the most morally upright and well-intentioned individual. The stakes are so incredibly high. The federal government has grown so large and the regulatory agencies so powerfully controlling, the political party holding power over either the House or the Senate can reap enormous sums for its members from lobbyists. In the winter of 2014 when Comcast Corporation agreed to buy Time Warner Cable, the front-page story was all about whether the Comcast CEO had spent enough money in the past five years buying access and influence in the White House, Congress, and the Federal Communications Commission regulating his industry.[39] Growth of Comcast depends entirely on the approval of those in power. In late 2013, JP Morgan Chase agreed to a $13 billion settlement with the justice department for alleged wrongdoing by two distressed institutions acquired at the behest of the US government, which allegedly unlawful behavior occurred before the bank acquired these institutions. The reason given by the CEO was to avoid the enormous cost in dollars, man hours, and years of management distraction defending the bank against the federal government.

Senators and congressmen suddenly become very, very wealthy. Tens of millions of dollars are spent on congressional and Senate elections. Hundreds of millions are spent on the presidency because the White House rules the bureaucracies and can grant economic favors or wreak economic ruin on any industry in the national economy. A divided Congress makes the presidency ever more powerful because the president wields dictatorial power unless Congress passes a law to stop the administration. If the president's party holds one house of Congress, the president is ruler of all. Demagogues begin to rise to the top. And campaigns focus on slandering one's opponent. We are now in an era of politics of destruction.

National issues no longer matter. It is now all about power. The financial rewards for control of the federal regulatory apparatus are truly unlimited. Such major priorities for the American people as national security, the national debt, the rule of law, and global leadership are of little concern to the political elite. The only priority is to obtain and maintain power by any means for the incredible personal wealth that can be garnered.

The Run-up: 2006-2014

A House Divided

In 2004, the American people gave control of the Senate to the Democrats, and in 2006, they gave control of the House to the Democrats as well. In 2008, a Democrat president was elected, and the nation would be ruled by Democrats solely for the next two years. The political campaigns were viciously destructive. Negative campaign ads far outnumbered candidate issue advocacy ads. The politics of destruction was firmly established, and the battle lines were drawn. As in war, the parties were staffed for conflict, not compromise.

In 2009, a new Democrat Congress rubber-stamped the new president's grand stimulus package of over one trillion dollars to favored constituencies who might be adversely affected by the national economic downturn. The national debt and deficit soared. A new grassroots movement developed among alarmed conservative citizens who railed against the huge stimulus and bailouts of banks and General Motors, increasing the national debt. These so-called Tea Party Patriots grew significantly in popularity after the passage by the Democrats of the national health-care law in early 2010. The result was a change in control of the House in 2010 elections with the Tea Party Patriots joining the ranks of the Republican Party.

The House passed budgets and appropriation bills which are its prerogative under the Constitution. The Senate majority leader would not bring any of these bills to the floor of the Senate for debate or action. The Democrat view has been since 2010 that the people made a silly mistake by electing Republicans to the House. They will just wait until the people get tired of this silliness and elect Democrats again.

Meanwhile, the Central Authority is on autopilot, and the national debt soars. From 2000 to 2006, the national debt grew $2.8 trillion (50 percent) from $5.7 trillion to $8.5 trillion under the Republicans. From 2006 to 2012, the national debt grew another

$7.5 trillion (88 percent) to $16 trillion under the Democrats. Congress did nothing. The pace of growth in the national debt is increasing. It was at a level equal to 99 percent of gross domestic product by 2013 when it exceeded $17 trillion. Congress has not been able to do anything about this ominous threat to our national security and national well-being.

The most significant division, however, was becoming apparent in the states. In 2010, we witnessed the great urban/rural divide and the great divide among the states. The Old South, the Great Plains, and the Mountain West turned very red with Republican governors and legislatures, while the North, East, and West Coasts remained Democrat blue. The battleground lay in the urbanized Great Lakes region. Michigan, Ohio, Indiana, and Wisconsin turned red Republican on the state government level but remained mixed in Congress. This division in geography by community and local government is the division most likely to auger for a Last Election.

A Grand Bargain that Failed

In February 2010, the president by executive order created the National Commission on Fiscal Responsibility and Reform, naming two statesmen, former Republican senator Alan Simpson and former Clinton White House chief of staff Erskine Bowles as cochairs. The two men issued their sixty-eight-page report on December 1, 2010, titled "A Moment of Truth." As a preamble, the report stated, "Our nation is on an unsustainable path. Spending is rising and revenues are falling short, requiring the government to borrow huge sums each year to make up the difference. We face staggering deficits."[40]

Their report was a grand plan to reduce discretionary spending, entitlement spending, and health-care spending while raising revenue through a combination of tax rate reduction and elimination of special tax deductions. The plan would reduce federal debt from 70 percent of projected GDP in 2015 to 40 percent of GDP in 2035. Reform was comprehensive, and its objectives were reasonably achievable. It had elements both agreeable and objectionable to both political parties. Compromise was necessary.

The Republican controlled House was amenable to a grand plan since it was passing its own comprehensive deficit reduction budgets that died in the Senate. The Democrat controlled Senate was the problem. Recognizing this political reality, a so-called Gang of Six senior senators, three Republicans and three Democrats, formed a group to work through their own plan to present to the Senate. The Gang of Six produced their own plan which looked a lot like Simpson-Bowles. It was more of a road map to reform elements that would need to be considered by the various Senate committees. Nothing happened in the Senate.[41]

As a ploy to require action on deficit reduction, the House was refusing to agree to a raise in the debt limit in the summer of 2011, and an agreement was struck with the president and Congress to require a sequester of $1 trillion in spending across the board on January 1, 2013, if Congress failed to act on deficit reduction. This would get the president past his 2012 reelection bid. And it was thought that a sequester was so disagreeable to both political parties, a compromise would be forged. But the divide was so great, no grand bargain was achieved, and the sequestration began in 2013.

Stop Gap Measures

The federal government is operating on autopilot. The Senate did not approve an annual budget from 2009 through 2013. In 2012, the House passed seven appropriation bills, which were approved by the Senate Appropriations Committee and sent to the full Senate for action. But the majority leader would not bring them to a vote. In order to keep the federal government running, one-month, two-month, and six-month short-term spending authority has been required since 2009. The Democrats bet that the Republicans must approve this spending or be blamed for shutting down the government. The Republican frustration did cause such action in the fall of 2013, and sure enough, the media blamed them solely. So periodically the debt ceiling is raised and the spending pattern continues to be authorized. Finally, to get through the 2014 election, an actual budget resolution was passed by Congress in the fall of 2013, which continues the spending rise and deficit and increase in debt.

A Bad Law Makes Matters Worse

In a hopelessly divided and increasingly rancorous America, the Democrats took advantage of their moment of total control in 2009 to pass sweeping legislation to nationalize the entire health-care system in the United States without a single member of the other party in support. No one in Congress actually knew what was in the law that ran over one thousand pages. The Democrat Speaker blurted out in debate, "We have to pass it first to find out what is in it." This law is not the tipping point. That has already occurred. This law may well prove to be the catalyst for the Last Election.

By early 2014, Americans know that the promises made by the president and advocates of the law were not only false but known to be false at the time they were made. The American people were hoodwinked. Over 20 percent of the national economy is being converted to a federal government program in which bureaucrats under the control of the political party in the White House will determine who gets medical care, what choice, if any, they may have of doctors or hospitals, how long they have to wait for the care they seek, and what this service will cost them in fees, taxes, fines, and liens on their assets. These same bureaucrats will control the use of drugs, the creation of new drugs (through approval process and reimbursement of cost), and the use and creation of medical devices, medical equipment, and medical supplies. The market for this enormous industry will be determined by a few men and women in Washington. The utterly imperative need for access to these incredibly powerful federal officials will spawn a whole new multibillion-dollar industry of lavish influence peddling, further corrupting our society and crippling our nation's economy. The personal disruptions, personal stress, suffering of pain, and death to those left out or abused in the process may indeed make Bleeding Kansas seem mild by comparison.

The Division Intensifies

Both the Republican and Democrat parties have been changing materially since the millennium. The Democrats are increasingly devoted to a Way of Life dominated by government direction and care. Wealth is created by influencing government to direct activity and funds to your enterprise. Power is maintained by influencing the masses with media messaging focused on fear and anger directed to others who may threaten your power with their ideas. The Republicans are increasingly focused on limiting the reach of national power over their lives and staunching the enormous increase in national debt which threatens all savings of the people. Power is maintained by influencing the masses to the dangers of unlimited government and the opportunities presented by more personal freedom.

Fear, anger, and the politics of destruction are winning the game. The Republicans have no answer to this destructive onslaught supported by the national media. Republicans have no real vision of a Way of Life starkly different from the Democrats. Republicans would just like the Democrats to tone it down, take a

110 James Glenn Reynolds

breather, let us all catch up. Let's all be reasonable and get along. The Republicans don't really understand how to operate in an era ruled by the politics of destruction, but they sure did have a hand in bringing it on.

Beginning officially in 2009 after the bailouts of Wall Street and General Motors followed by the grand stimulus of $1 trillion, a new grassroots political movement developed calling themselves the Tea Party Patriots. Their mission is fiscal responsibility, constitutionally limited government, and free market economic policies. Passage of the national health-care law in March 2010 drew millions of Americans into the Tea Party Movement to voice their disapproval of this law. During town meetings and political rallies that year, the Tea Party citizens would not be shouted down. They rose up and asserted themselves. The Democrats lost their majority in the House, and new members sympathetic to the Tea Party joined the ranks of the new Republican majority.

Once again we had a divided government, and the division was now much more rancorous. The national media ridiculed the Tea Party, much as the Free Soilers were ridiculed as kooks in the early 1850s. Tea Party Patriots have a vision of a Way of Life that is the polar opposite of the prevailing Democrat Way of Life. The Tea Party Patriots are a small minority, but much like the abolitionist Free Soilers, their passion is their strength. They exist in every community but particularly in the red states. They are not interested in power. Their passion is for freedom and a Way of Life free of laws governing so many aspects of human activity.

The Tea Party movement is not going away because its members are alarmed citizens. The alarm will likely intensify as the national debt grows, the intrusion of the Central Authority on everyday life intensifies, and our standard of living declines. The lines are now drawn.

The Supreme Court Is No Help

The national health-care law is arguably causing the greatest amount of aggravation among a divided people. The law was considered by many to be clearly unconstitutional because it mandated human activity. Congress has the power under the Constitution to regulate interstate commerce but not to mandate it. For those failing to comply with this mandated action, the law assesses a penalty in the form of a fine which becomes a lien against one's income and assets. The National Federation of Independent Business challenged the law and was supported by attorneys general in over half the states. Surprisingly, Chief Justice Roberts joined the liberal wing of the court, resulting in a 5-4 decision upholding the law as constitutional.[42] Roberts's convoluted reasoning was that the penalty could be considered by the court to be a tax which Congress has authority to levy on human inactivity. He reasoned that what Congress has no power to regulate or mandate, it can nevertheless tax. The Supreme Court ignored statutory language stating that the penalty is not a tax.

Justice Roberts obviously holds the view that the court cannot thwart the advance of the socialist welfare state if that is indeed what representatives of the people wish to cause to occur.

The Constitution does not protect individual liberty if the Central Authority wishes to tax any inaction or other behavior it finds unbecoming. So one must buy health insurance, and one must buy health insurance in the form of a plan approved by the Central Authority, or else. Else means to be taxed, and there is evidently no limit to the amount of tax that might be levied.

There are a number of ways to bring someone into bondage. Certainly one method is to assess economic penalties in the form of fines to force conforming behavior. The Supreme Court is not going to prevent this sort of event from occurring if it is the will of Congress. The court essentially held that nine men and women cannot control the will of the majority, even if that will creates an America far, far different from that contemplated in the Constitution. If the minority view is to prevail, that view must grow into a majority. Otherwise it may be vanquished by the majority. If we are to be saved from a Last Election, it will not be the Supreme Court coming to our rescue.

The Absence of Leadership

A divided nation produces weak leaders. Since 1988, we have had a series of unremarkable presidents. George Bush (41) kicked Iraq out of Kuwait and didn't finish the job in Baghdad. He said he wouldn't raise taxes but promptly did so, bringing on a recession, leaving him with just one term in office. Clinton was elected with less than a majority vote, thanks to third-party candidate Ross Perot.

Clinton really liked being president, accommodated the opposition, kept defense light, enjoyed an economic boom and a short-lived surplus. Women still love him, but his presidency is marked more by controversial behavior in the White House than anything else.

George Bush (43) was our reluctant president, needed the Supreme Court to declare him the winner, was stunned by the terrorist attacks and over-influenced by his advisers, went to war, and told the American people to go shopping. He declared victory when there was none and won reelection by destroying his opposition with negative advertising. The current president is the weakest of all, detaching himself from responsibility for both foreign and domestic affairs and lecturing us incessantly about our collective failings.

The only president during this twenty-six-year period to be effective in governing was Clinton who forged a working relationship with the other party in Congress. Americans deride their government, but they are far too evenly divided to be effectively led.

Since 2006, both political parties have installed a weak Speaker of the House and a weak majority leader in the Senate. In times of division and rancor, no member or senator wishes to be led.

As a result, cohesive action in the national Congress becomes virtually impossible. In the Senate, the leader protects his party from difficult decisions on votes by simply preventing bills from coming to the floor for a vote. In the House, weak Speakers cannot lead their party caucuses but are rather driven by them.

In the Republican controlled House of Representatives, the Speaker cannot forge a majority of his party to pass a compromise federal budget, so he has to solicit the Democrats to join with the moderate wing of his party to produce a majority. He is unable to lead his own party in the direction he believes to be proper.

The Democrat leadership in the Senate is so ineffective that the majority found it necessary to destroy the two-hundred-year-old sixty-vote requirement for its advise and consent function in approving political appointees and judges. The leadership could not convince the Democrat administration to appoint more centrist individuals that could muster the sixty votes. The easy way out was to destroy this consensus-forging rule, further alienating nearly 50 percent of its members.

Weak leadership cannot forge consensus. The nation is a ship adrift in unstable seas with no strong hand at the helm, a divisive and rebellious crew, and a hapless core of officers. Oh, dear.

Inevitable Conflict

In the United States of today, there are no great compromises to be had. The growth of the Central Authority seems unstoppable, creating the image of a monster trudging along, trampling random humanity in its path. The Northeast and West Coast states seem unperturbed, even embracing this monster. The elite benefit greatly from the monster's largess and believe it can actually be kept tame with constant feeding of money into its gaping jaws. In 2013, over $3.2 billion was spent on Washington lobbyists.[43] The biggest global customer to be influenced is the Central Authority, either by award of contract for purchase of services and products or by award of a rule that will require everyone else to buy the product or service. The two stroke each other with the people's money.

The blue states have a majority of the people and the votes. To win those votes and maintain power, the Central Authority in collaboration with the financial elite pays out cash, delivers services, and creates rights to draw the underclass into bondage. The Supreme Court will not intervene to restrain the majority. The Constitution is an old document no longer of much relevance.

A new ethic has been crafted by the Central Authority and financial elite to justify this social regimen, developed over the past fifty years. It is an ethic of benign imperial power of the intellectual elite to provide equality in all things, justice in the redistribution of property and income, freedom from want, and liberty in the form of individual rights to accept the Central Authority view of things.

The people are clearly better off under this social regimen because they cannot be trusted to care for themselves. They are far too ignorant, far too weak, and far too helpless to avoid temptation, save for their future, and make a better life. The Democrats are saving the people from the barbarians who would exploit them. The national media, populated by people who seek influence and a measure of power, are in collaboration. And in Washington, DC, there has not been a recession since 1963. Life is good for the Central Authority and its friends.

The lie in this view of our Way of Life is revealed when the prevailing Central Authority power is threatened by opposing views. The red states do not have the people to secure a balance of power, let alone to gain power nationally. But there are currently, since 2010, a sufficient number of people and their representatives inclined to resist the growth of the Central Authority. When the sequester of government growth in spending became a reality at the end of 2012 due to the inability of Congress to come to an alternative compromise, the Central Authority issued threats and dire warnings of the chaos that would ensue, particularly in air travel, but also in food inspection, border control, and national security. In essence, the Central Authority meant to penalize the American people for daring to question its power to rule.

Earlier in 2012, the Central Authority launched investigations of conservative groups who were raising money to influence the 2012 electoral process and blocked their rightful exemptions from taxation, all to intimidate and successfully suppress dissenting views. This outrageous behavior by the IRS was encouraged and even demanded by the president and Democrat senate leaders on no less than a dozen occasions in speeches and letters. Applications for exemption were unlawfully leaked to liberal media outlets. When threatened by the very legitimate electoral process, the

Central Authority is capable of vicious action against its fellow citizens.

In 2013, the Supreme Court soberly ruled that fifty-year-old rules requiring southern states to seek approval of the Central Authority to change voting laws were no longer a necessary or proper interference with state government. The Central Authority's response has been to sue both Texas and North Carolina to prevent changes in laws to require a picture identification to vote, challenging the Supreme Court to rule again and hoping perhaps to win an election with fraudulent voting before the court has the opportunity to rule.

The stakes in each election are now so incredibly high because the power of the Central Authority is so enormous, civil order and decorum are lost to the politics of total destruction. In 2012, $7 billion ($7,000,000,000) was spent to elect a president, one third of the Senate, and members of the House, an amount more than double that of the highly contested Bush/Gore election in 2000.[44] In 2014, we will have another election of the House and a third of the Senate. Nothing of consequence will be decided in the nation by this election except which individuals and groups will have more or less control of the Central Authority and the power to enrich themselves.

The Supreme Court, as an equal branch of government, is no longer equal nor of much use in protecting the minority population. We learned in the 1850s that the court's ruling to protect the minority slaveholders under the Constitution, as was their right and the court's duty, was an utterly ineffective act. The majority of people were moving away from acceptance of this institution and would not be limited by the Constitution's requirements for a super majority to amend its provisions. The majority set out to destroy the minority in a civil war. The Supreme Court was powerless to stop it.

Today the court has come to realize, perhaps in part because of its knowledge of our history in the 1850s, that it cannot prevent the majority from bringing all the people into bondage at its will. Better perhaps to let the mob have its way rather than to rebuke the mob and invite a civil war. Sadly, though, failure to invoke the power of the Constitution to restrain the mob will inevitably lead us to a Last Election and the uncertain future that follows.

Much has been written in the past several years concerning the ominous growth of viciously destructive political discourse. The politics of destruction is the politics of absolute control and absolute power. The stakes would have to be very, very high to justify this level of effort and financial investment. By 1860, it was utterly clear to all in the South that the Northern people intended to destroy the institution of slavery and destroy the Southern Way of Life. In 2014, the Central Authority may indeed be large enough now to be perceived as possessing essentially absolute and unlimited power to destroy any way of life inconsistent with its Way of Life.

For example, the Occupational Safety and Health Administration (OSHA) is banned by federal law from jurisdiction over small family farms with fewer than ten nonfamily employees. However, OSHA is concerned about grain-storage bins because workers in grain-storage businesses have suffered injury or death while working on storage machinery and in the confined space within a storage bin. OSHA decides it needs to be sure all uses of these bins nationwide are regulated by its rules for grain-storage businesses. The agency concludes that farm operations cease at harvest, and that family farms may in fact be engaged in a number of businesses subject to OSHA regulation. Therefore, a family farm with one employee that has a couple of storage bins for its produce is in fact in the grain-storage business and subject to OSHA regulations and fines. Without notice, OSHA entered a Nebraska farm, discovered several violations of its rules for regulated businesses, and fined the farm family $132,000. No one had complained or had been injured. OSHA invaded another small farmer in Ohio. Small farmers do not have the financial resources to fight OSHA or any other federal regulatory agency when it extends its power unlawfully. Fortunately, the farmers questioned this surprise assault, Senators were apprised, and eventually OSHA backed down.[45]

Farmers are abused by one agency, small businesses are abused by several agencies, petroleum and coal producers are abused by another agency, small communities, sheriffs, and state governments are abused by the justice department. Governor Perry of Texas declared in 2012 that "We are at war with the federal government." He was merely stating a fact, as he saw the situation in Texas.

By 1860, the political discourse of hate and destruction had been a routine ethic for over ten years, whereas in 2014 this awful state has only been fully apparent since the Democrats and their collectivist elite realized in 2010 that they did not control America as completely as they wished or thought they did. The time for separation is not yet upon us, though it is fast approaching. We know the national debt is soaring and will crush us in due time. We know there will be a reckoning. We also know that we disagree on many aspects of life, and that on these matters we are hopelessly divided.

But we have not yet concluded that we have two distinct and utterly incompatible Ways of Life. Our political and business leaders continue to behave as though there is some strong common thread that binds us together as one people. Yet if the common thread is but an illusion, the path to separation opens wide and beckons.

Fraying the Common Thread

For nearly two centuries, historians and politicians have been attempting to define the American, the American experience, and the American culture. Common to most of these attempts are the concepts of (1) social organization through democratic institutions honoring individual liberty, equal opportunity, and equal justice; (2) a high level of civic participation; (3) protection of private property and the celebration of hard work; and (4) marriage, family, and religiosity.

American culture was essentially the European culture of the white race transplanted to a new continent with new ideals of social organization. To become truly American, though, one had to loose the shackles of tradition, class, and habit that bound Europeans to limitations. Tocqueville observed in the 1830s that "in most of the operations of the mind, each American appeals to the individual exercise of his own understanding alone."[46]

There were numerous communities and regions throughout America that attracted men and women of similar nationalities and religions, as these two characteristics defined culture. People gravitate to the familiar, particularly in a new physical environment. In many of these communities, the old traditions and language were preserved to provide the comfort of familiarity while assimilation into the new American culture steadily advanced. Yet nearly everyone did assimilate.

Everyone knew what it meant to be an American. It meant the opportunity to work hard, earn property, and keep what you earned for the benefit of you and your family. There was no equality in life and little equality of opportunity. Fairness was expected of the judge, and hopefully your neighbor, but not much beyond that. Nevertheless, it was better here than anywhere else. Everyone knew it. Everyone went to work. And everyone melted into this pot fairly quickly, often in the span of one generation.

There are many common threads bound together and running through this culture. Most have been discussed, including the work ethic, the rule of law, and private property rights. In addition, the individual freedoms and those left to the states in the Bill of Rights are of significance in our common culture. We spoke and wrote one official language, English. And although Tocqueville observed that we spent no time on philosophy or formal education,[47] we did indeed have a very strong common thread on the philosophy of moral and social life bound up in one book, the Bible. Later in our history, we shared in common our pursuit of adventure, conquest, and settlement of this great land and, in the twentieth century, shared our common pursuit of empire.

These many common threads did not really apply to the black race brought here against their will as slaves. Nor did it apply to the native Indian population. Our common culture really was not common among all humans living here. We were never a homogeneous people. Those who could not or would not assimilate were left largely forgotten by the wayside. The plight of these peoples continues to haunt our society to this day and continues to tear at what common threads may remain.

Yet perhaps what haunts us most these days is the shared understanding of how different we are or have become. During the last twenty-five years, historians, journalists, and other observers have been actively engaged in writing about these differences. One recent well-researched book by writer Colin Woodard recounts the history of eleven nations of North America.[48] The author defines a nation as "a group of people who share—or believe they share—a common culture, ethnic origin, language, historical experience, artifacts, and symbols."[49] He has discovered no less than eleven of these nations from the Mexican border to the Arctic Circle. The geographic contortions of his map look like a well-gerrymandered series of congressional districts. And of these nations, the author asserts in his introduction, "Few have shown any indication that they are melting into some sort of unified American culture. On the contrary, since 1960 the fault lines between these nations have been growing wider, fueling culture wars, constitutional struggles, and ever more frequent pleas for unity."[50]

Somehow, Tocqueville missed all this during his wanderings in the early nineteenth century. He was observing and trying to understand this radically new form of social organization. Certainly he was well aware of the various cultural differences of the peoples that immigrated to America, and he had difficulty defining the common thread, but in his observations, it is clear that he knew one existed because the Americans he met seemed to know. Woodard would have us understand that we never had a common culture. I think Woodard is missing a common historical thread and that indeed Tocqueville observed us correctly. But that was then.

The truth is that even if we did at one time enjoy a common thread in our many cultures, not much remains, and this fact lies at the heart of our national dysfunction. Politicians wistfully refer to America as an idea, not a place or a people. We are the embodiment of some idea of freedom and a beacon of light for everyone to look up to with little or no definition of the idea or the light. The notion of American exceptionalism, once a rationale for purposeful, confident action, has been disparaged as a form of cultural arrogance offensive to other cultures. We prefer to dwell on our inadequacies and flail ourselves for past failures. We have become ashamed of our history.

Our current notions of America do not call us to action unless it is personal consumption to keep the economy going. An identity that requires no action in defense or furtherance of it is not a very powerful identity. It is not an identity that has the power to unify, provide guidance, or compel loyalty. It is an identity that just is, mushy and ephemeral.

We have found that a large Central Authority is not a large central ethic. It is simply a monster to be coped with by each feudal community. Yet it is not the national government destroying our central ethic. It is each of us, either by design or by acquiescence.

Arthur Schlesinger Jr. observed in his 1992 book that multiculturalism inculcated by the intellectual elite in our secondary and university education was disuniting America.[51] By then, some twenty years ago, graduation requirements of 78 percent of American universities did not require a course in western civilization.[52] It is much worse today when even courses in American history are not required. Instead, the curriculum is about learning racial or ethnic identity from professors who would have us learn their idea of history, not what actually happened. As Schlesinger notes, "The debate about the curriculum is a debate about what it means to be an American."[53] This debate has largely been won by those who would remake the American culture by replacing our European values with those of non-Western cultures. The great universities of our national culture have wholeheartedly embraced this change.

Schlesinger, the historian, implored us to teach and learn the history that is uniquely ours. It may not be better than others, but it is better for us because it defines who we are, why we came here, what we believed in that drove us here and to be together. "Above all, history can give a sense of national identity. We don't have to believe that our values are absolutely better than the next fellow's or the next country's, but we have no doubt that they are better for us, reared as we are—and are worth living by and worth dying for."[54]

I recall vividly a conversation around the Thanksgiving table in West Barrington, Rhode Island, in 1980. The women and younger children had moved away to another part of the home, leaving my host and me with our two early teen sons at the table. The subject under discussion was the late Oregon senator Mark Hatfield's proposal of unilateral nuclear disarmament. My host, then chairman of Brown University Medical School, was a Brit influenced by the recent past. His brilliant son was attending an exclusive private school. My son was in public school locally. The discussion had proceeded for some time when my host's son interrupted to assert, "Well, there is nothing worth dying for." To which my son retorted, "If there is nothing worth dying for, there is nothing worth living for." My host and I looked at one another and rose from the table without another word.

My son today is a global executive, influenced by some forty odd years of life in the United States. I wonder what his reaction would be today. I haven't asked him about this lately. But it seems to me that without our history, without our common memory, we are easy prey for the demagogues and charlatans and relativists. What are we willing to die for these days?

For over one hundred years following the Civil War, the great migrations to America settled in their ethnic enclaves to make a new life, gradually learning the English language and assimilating the American culture. America was their new home, whether they settled in New York, Michigan, North Dakota, or

California. We all learned the same history from the same books. Our curriculum defined us. History is our national memory. We all shared the same memory. This common understanding of our history taught in one language prepared us to defend our nation successfully in two great world wars and to build the greatest empire to ever exist on earth. Now the revisionists say, "Shame on us!" Our teachers have taken away our story and replaced it with another story more to their liking.

Schlesinger observed that by 1992, "The ethnic revolt against the melting pot has reached the point, in rhetoric at least, though not I think in reality, of a denial of the idea of a common culture and a single society. If large numbers of people really accept this, the republic would be in serious trouble."[55] We now have twenty more years of teaching anything but our common history, twenty more years of ethnic and racial centeredness, and twenty more years of debasing our Western European values.

Schlesinger didn't say what would happen after we got in "serious trouble." We are much nearer to finding out. Having killed the empire, rejected our heritage, and debased our history, we are now withdrawing to our core communities and ignoring our national identity.

Yet our national government is not ignoring us. Rather it is increasingly and incessantly intrusive in every aspect of life without the moral imperative of national joy or shared national mission. The federal government Central Authority is crowding out our regional heritage by nullifying our laws and making national rules for us all. We are drawing nearer to a catharsis.

We are now a beset people in a large portion of the nation geographically and occupationally. The great collectivist elite do not understand this fact or prefer to ignore it in favor of its agenda for us all. The elite are not beset because they are in control. There is nothing new in this state of affairs. It has always been thus. Eventually, though, the besetting gets too overwhelming where there are no effective limits on those in power. Our Central Authority is now so powerful and intrusive, it touches and oppresses nearly everyone.

The great disconnect between the collectivist elite and everyone else was highlighted recently by one of their premier darlings, and a pretty smart guy to be sure, Thomas Friedman, who with his pal, Michael Mandelbaum, gave us their own modern-day book of lamentations.[56] They first identify our four great societal challenges, the first three of which are their hobby horses of adapting to globalization, adjusting to the information technology revolution, and managing the rise in energy consumption and threat to the environment. The fourth challenge is "how to cope with the large and soaring budget deficits."[57] The only challenge of the four that is high on most Americans' lists is the soaring debt which many believe needs an action verb stronger than "to cope."

Friedman and Mandelbaum then observe the obvious, "What all four of these challenges have in common is that they require a collective response. They are too big to be addressed by one party alone, or by one segment of the public."[58]

So there we have it. The collectivist elite defines society's priorities in a way to require, and therefore justify, an enormous Central Authority that the elite can influence and hopefully control through the exercise of their powerful and superior intellect to provide us a life and a territory to live in that we are incapable of figuring out on our own or in smaller communities.

The disconnect, unfortunately, goes much, much deeper. Friedman and Mandelbaum assert that America's prosperity rests on the "five pillars" of public education, public financing of infrastructure, government support of immigration, government support for basic research, and government regulation of private sector economic activity.[59]

"Throughout our history these five pillars have made it possible for Americans to apply their individual energies, their talents, and their entrepreneurial drive to make themselves, and their country, richer and more powerful."[60]

What history books did these men read? Ford and Sloan built automobiles before there were roads, not afterward. We didn't develop the interstate highway system until the automobile industry was a half-century old. Edison did his work without any infrastructure. The success of inventions was financed by private risk takers like J. P. Morgan, not government largess. The high-stakes gamblers who managed to finance and build the intercontinental railroad from San Francisco to Promontory Point would likely differ with the assertions of Friedman and Mandelbaum.

There was no public education to speak of as we were building the empire. Trades were learned by apprenticeships. Inventions sprang from this learning. There was no regulation of economic activity except rules to facilitate, not restrain, commerce. Immigration was not a pillar of prosperity except for the immigrants who came here to be free and build a new life absent oppressive governmental authority. The two pillars of prosperity fostered by government were protection of private property and the rule of law. Somehow Friedman and Mandelbaum missed these.

The government did provide land and lots of it to those willing to brave the interior to build homes, farms, ranches, mines, and transportation, but infrastructure financing was sparse until the welfare dams of the 1930s putting men back to work.

Then came World War II, the Cold War aftermath, and the great growth of the military/industrial complex that alarmed Eisenhower. We used the wealth of empire to create government-financed research, which eventually crowded out much of the privately financed research and leaves us dependent today on the Central Authority.

Friedman quotes the late senator Daniel Patrick Moynihan who said, "Everyone is entitled to his own opinion but not his own facts." We can all lament to some degree the amount of factual rubbish distributed in the unedited Internet, but far more destructive to the body politic is the choice of facts deployed by the elite to justify their opinions because they have the power to do so, and their choices rule us all. Friedman and Mandelbaum have organized their facts to suit their view of the world and our society. Historian Niall Ferguson and other historians do so also, as do I in this writing, and does every person who forms an opinion from observation and research.

The crucial observation here is the enormous chasm that lies between us in our choices, the opinions that flow from those choices, and the consequences that will likely ensue. Friedman observes the principal consequence but misinterprets it as an example of the decline in respect for authority. He tells the story of a professor of soil science who is visiting with an old cattleman that has been relegated by his sons to blueberry farming. The professor wants to buy some plants, and in the conversation, the subject of climate change comes up. The old man "doesn't believe in any of that stuff" and declines an offer from the soil scientist to educate him on the subject, saying that he was "happy with his opinions." The soil scientist's observation is, "Great guy . . . but just not interested."[61]

Friedman sees this story as an example of the ebbing respect for authority and expertise, but when I read the story, I felt I knew this man. He just wants to be left alone. His response was a good way to cut off the conversation and save himself from a disagreeable argument. For all we know, the old former cattleman might have been an expert himself. Some guy wants to buy some plants and tell the old man how he should feel about climate change along the way? Frankly, I'm just not interested. Give it a rest already.

The consequence of this onslaught is our decision to simply seek refuge. We might be angry, but anger is an exhausting emotion. We are not able to do our work to provide ourselves a livelihood and be angry all the time. We don't have enough energy. Nor do we have the energy to withstand seemingly constant unsolicited confrontations by the controlling Central Authority with their experts and their police. We seek refuge in a number of ways. We tune out the conversation. We refuse to engage. We don't try to figure out what is truth, what facts are relevant, and what the real agenda is. We're on overload. "Gimme Shelter," sang the Rolling Stones.

Unfortunately, there is little shelter left to us. The 10 percenters are working overtime and very effectively. With the Central Authority now in a position to control nearly all human activity, the task at hand is to influence the Central Authority to work the will of the special interest 10 percent (or less) group. The regulatory process of rule making in the enabling laws passed by Congress requires often a rigorous fact-finding investigation which takes time and runs the risk of disarming the cause of the special interest. This process can be used to political advantage by both proponents and opponents. The interminable delay of approval of the Keystone pipeline from Canada to Texas is an example of Central Authority delay to thwart the fossil fuel industry and support the environmental lobby. And elections are important because they determine who gets to make the rules and run the Central Authority bureaus.

But even when the person with the correct attitude is not able to accomplish a task at hand with dispatch, there is another effective method to reach the special interest goal. Simply sue the Central Authority agency that is not doing what you wish. For example, the Environmental Protection Agency (EPA) wants to shut down the coal industry but is having difficulty getting new rules through the administrative rule-making process to accomplish this goal. However, the EPA does have authority without oversight to settle a lawsuit by agreeing to implement new rules. So we should look for one or more environmental lobbies to sue the EPA alleging that the agency is not complying properly with its mandate under the Clean Air Act. The two parties will then settle the case with the EPA agreeing to comply with the plaintiff's demands. The case never goes to trial because neither party wants either the expense or the burden of proving the legal justification for the mutually desired outcome. A judge signs off on the settlement, effectively subverting and bypassing the administrative rule-making process. Friendly federal judges are in abundance. And there is no aggrieved party to appeal the judgment.

A small special interest with lots of money can work its will with a sympathetic Central Authority bent on more and more control.

The so-called sue-and-settle racket is used most frequently by the Sierra Club (thirty-four times), Wild Earth Guardians (twenty), Natural Resources Defense Council (nine), Center for Biological Diversity (six), and Environmental Defense Fund (five), according to a US Chamber of Commerce study report published in May 2013.[62] Unsurprisingly, most of the cases are brought in the wilderness of Washington, DC, or San Francisco. Both advocacy groups (the 10 percenters) and industry groups have used the tactic, but the most egregious cases involve new rule making under the Clean Air Act regulating utilities and the Endangered Species Act regulating land use and development.

In 2011, the Fish and Wildlife Service settled two friendly cases, agreeing to put 720 new candidates on the endangered species list, thus driving FWS to spend the money and devote the time required by such designation to investigate this large new crop of potential roadblocks to be used by the green lobby to prevent development or discovery and use of fossil fuels. In that year, over 75 percent of Fish and Wildlife's budget for endangered species and critical habitat was spent on actions required by court orders or settlement agreements. A very small minority is thus able to rule all of us in our homes, farms, and factories by controlling the work of the Central Authority.

Popular columnist Peggy Noonan, who has a gifted way with words, wrote the following in her March 1, 2014, column in the *Wall Street Journal*:

> There are few areas of national life left in which *the progressive left* are not busy, and few in which they're not making it worse. There are always more regulations, fees and fiats, always more cultural pressure and insistence . . . I think a lot of people right now . . . feel like a guy in a batting cage taking ball after ball from an automatic pitching machine. He's hitting the ball and keeping up and suddenly the machine starts going berserk. It's firing five balls a second, then 10. At first he tries to hit a few. Then he's just trying to duck, trying not to get hurt . . . People feel beset because they are. All these things are pieces of a larger, bullying ineptitude. And people know, they are aware.

Conservatives sometimes feel exhausted from trying to fight back on a million fronts. A leftist might say: "yes, that's the plan."

But the left too is damaged. They look hollowed out and incoherent. Their victories, removed of meaning, are only the triumphs of small aggressions. They win the day but not the era. The result is not progress but more national division, more of a grinding sense of dislike. At first it will be aimed at the progressive left, but in time it will likely be aimed at America itself, or rather America as It Is Now. When the progressive left wins, they will win, year by year, less of a country.

The Central Authority is no longer restricted in its activity by the rule of law. I have cited several examples and could cite many, many more. There is no refuge for the citizen. The Central Authority will go where it chooses. If the law does not permit, the Central Authority will redefine the law to its liking. The national health-care law is not really a law but a license to the Central Authority to organize, operate, regulate, and mandate the health care (or lack thereof) for every citizen.

Is there any refuge, then, from the bombardment of rule making by those in the Central Authority who would direct all aspects of our lives, including what we think and what we are allowed to say? Is this the new freedom that is to be ours in America? This can't really be the essence of life, now, can it?

The Essence of Life

In the 1992 presidential election campaign, then candidate William Jefferson Clinton proclaimed the essence of life in the following phrase, "It's the economy, stupid." Nothing else is really important, let alone decisive. And he may have been correct in his assessment of American life. Yet the economy is not the essence. Our work is vital to our self-esteem and well-being. The economy is important, but it is not the essence.

It's about life worth living, really. It's always been about life worth living. If we are all about the task of building this empire and rocketing forward, well, maybe all of us should climb on that train and worry about the rest of the stuff later. But if we are no longer on a bullet train but instead aboard a rudderless ship adrift at sea, and our debt is about to overwhelm us with ugly choices crashing on a looming reef; maybe we think about abandoning that ship to find that other life we left behind in our haste and exuberance.

For human beings, the essence of life worth living is ultimately about two fundamental human needs: home and faith. These two fundamental needs will be the root motivation for the Last Election. When one or both is violated to the extent beyond tolerance, beyond the point of refuge, the affected people will separate themselves officially from the force that encroached too far.

Home

When a US citizen returns to the United States and passes through passport control, the officer occasionally looks the returning citizen in the eye and says sincerely, "Welcome home." It is a special feeling to be welcomed home, to have arrived home, to be at home.

Is the United States of America really our home? Of course it is. We value our passport, cheer for our national teams, pledge allegiance to the flag, sing our national anthem, and . . . and . . . let's see . . . what else? Do we honor our heroes, or do we trash them with revisionist (enlightened) historical perspective? Do we study our history anymore? Do we adhere to our constitutional documents of limited government? Do we share one common language? Do we volunteer en masse to shoulder arms and stand in harm's way when our duty calls? When was the last time our leaders called us to this duty in large numbers? Called (drafted) US troops arrived in Vietnam in 1965. And how did we handle those next four years?

Home is a place more narrowly defined than America or the United States. Home is not just where the heart is. Home is the place you know and where

138

you are known. Home is where they have to take you in. Home is where you can dwell, where you can rest, close your eyes, and not be disoriented when you awaken. Home is where you can speak your mind or remain silent with acceptance. Home is without fear. Home is the place in which to be born and in which to live and to which to return to die.

In 1981, Joel Garreau, a *Washington Post* editor, published a very interesting book describing nine nations of North America, delineating by geography, culture, work, religion, and language the several identifiable regions that comprise this continent.[63] His marvelous work still sings a true song three decades later. His stories capture the soul of each region and the humanity that occupy that space. They are all gritty, real, and insightful about what differentiates us and where that happens and why. And more importantly they tell the tale of who we all really are.

One example is the poignant conversation the author had with Andrew Young Sr., a dentist and father of the congressman and UN ambassador of the same name, in his later years.

> Dr. Young, born in 1896, was a frail thoughtful man near the end of a long life when I talked with him. When he spoke about Dixie, he repeatedly came back to the point that, in his opinion:

> "The South has always been a better place to live than the North, even during segregation. You always knew where you were. The South

has always been better because you've had less chance of being embarrassed. In the North you could go into a store, or a tavern, but they'd serve you when they felt like serving you. In my opinion, it was better not to be able to go into a store at all than face that kind of humiliation. Now, in the South those unjust old laws don't exist. They can't hide behind those laws. In the North you still wait . . . Here in New Orleans, they meet you at the door."[64]

Few Americans outside of Dixie would believe this story let alone understand it. What is really important for us to know is how different we are in how we live, how we want to live, how we relate to one another and our place of living. In the vast Empty Quarter from New Mexico to the Arctic Circle, the people who inhabit that space wish to mine its resources for a living, not just coal, oil, gas, and uranium but trees, fish, and game. In Ecotopia running along the narrow coastal area from Santa Barbara to the Aleutians, don't you dare touch a twig or turn a rock. In Mexamerica, it is the Spanish language, not English, that binds. These stark differences provide the chemistry of separation, not unity.

In Garreau's words, "Forget the maze of state and provincial boundaries, those historical accidents and surveyors' mistakes. The reason no one except the trivia expert can name all fifty of the United States is that they hardly matter . . . Consider, instead, the way North America really works. It is Nine Nations."[65]

Garreau was on to something quite significant. But he either didn't know what it was or wasn't prepared to say. He mused, "If news, as has been observed elsewhere, is the first rough draft of history, and this book, at least partially, anticipates the news, then perhaps I'm in the disconcerting position of writing a book that will be more true when you read it than when I wrote it."[66]

Garreau closed his preface with the following:

> The final point to be made about thinking in regional terms is that, more often than not, it offers a reassuring view of the future.
>
> I do not think that North America is flying apart, or that it should.
>
> But I've spent some time talking to a University of Texas professor, a folklorist and regionalist, who does. For what it's worth, I'll pass on what he likes about Nine Nations.
>
> He thinks it shows that if Washington, D.C. were to slide into the Potomac tomorrow under the weight of its many burdens and crises, the result would be okay. The future would not be chaos; it would be a shift. North America would not suddenly look around to discover a strange and alien world. It would see a collection of healthy, powerful constituent parts that we've known all our lives—like Dixie. He sees Nine Nations as a resilient response of a tough people reaffirming their self-reliance. It's not

that social contracts are dissolving; it's just that the new ones are being born.

What he's saying, essentially, is that our values are separable from our regimes. We can preserve what is important to us, no matter what violence is done to the federal system, and the sooner we recognize that, the more confident of our future we'll be. This confidence, he adds, ironically may serve to bolster that very federal system.

I don't know. In some ways I think he's crazy. But this whole thing started as a kind of private craziness.[67]

When Garreau's book was published in 1981, the cultural separation was taking place as the unifying forces were beginning to crumble. The former was likely not caused by the latter but certainly enabled by it. The "mining mentality" of the Empty Quarter coexists peacefully with the "tree huggers" of Ecotopia if there is an overriding central ethic. We are all on the same page headed to our future together . . . or not.

Life's essence, from Joel Garreau,

Every North American knows a place . . . where, on your way back from your wanderings, surroundings stop feeling threatening, confusing, or strange. Ultimately, that's the reason we are Nine Nations. When you're from one, and you're in it, you know you're home.[68]

Whether we accept Garreau's nine nations and aberrations like Alaska, or we accept Woodard's convoluted eleven nations, or we make up our own, the reality of this exercise informs our understanding of what a map of North America might look like after the Last Election. The foundation is our home. Our community is formed within the boundary of life compatible with our home. Our community will likely be as large geographically as this feeling of compatibility will extend. Beyond that, we are forming human alliances of necessity and convenience.

As Garreau observed, these human alliances often encompass more than one of his nine nations. Texas, he argued, is three nations (Dixie on the east, Mexamerica to the southwest, and Breadbasket to the northwest) with all three fighting over the urban triangle formed by Dallas, Houston, and Austin.[69] If state governments are to exist in their current form, they must figure out the compatibility factor. States like Oklahoma, Kansas, Nebraska, and the Dakotas seem more stable as their urban centers remain culturally akin to their rural communities. But Texas, California, Oregon, Washington, and Colorado are all unstable as compatible social structures because they encompass regions with strikingly different concepts of home and the essence of life there.

As for the monster Central Authority of our federal government, there is no compatibility with home (except perhaps in the power corridor from Northern Virginia to Southwestern Connecticut). The Central Authority is no longer a convenience and may no longer be a necessity we are willing to abide. For many,

many Americans, the last time they responded to a call to join the collective effort and left their homes, farms, and factories to serve or vote for a national priority, they returned to their homes, farms, and factories to find the ATF, EEOC, EPA, FDA, HHS, INS, IRS, OSHA, and USDA (to name but a few) regulating some additional form of their daily activity.

What Friedman and Mandelbaum don't seem to be able to acknowledge is that our collective greatness does not emanate from the Central Authority but rather from our willingness to leave our homes, farms, and factories for a time to join together to meet an urgent national need in order to preserve those very homes, farms, and factories that we love so intensely. A beset people will not rise to the great challenges that require a collective response because they are worn-out, resentful, and increasingly disloyal to a Central Authority that continually oppresses their daily lives.

Defending the home, farm, and factory has risen to a new, heightened priority level. Our citizens are reevaluating their definition of home as they assess their neighbors, their communities, and their regional affiliations. The definition of home is narrowing. And our alienation with our national identity has grown beyond the tipping point.

If we lose our allegiance to home, we will all be lost to social chaos or human bondage. The salvation of human freedom is in our home as the core. We must preserve our home if we are to remain free. The only question, in the end, is whether we will choose to defend our home and demand freedom. The American people, in our many nations that we call home, continue to accept the United States of America as our alliance of convenience and necessity. But alas, it is not our home, if indeed it ever was. After the Last Election, new alliances of convenience and necessity will form, as they did in 1860. And they will form from the home as the core and the local community as the compatible extension of the core, all within these many nations on this North American continent.

Faith

The power of faith as a means of understanding the incomprehensible and knowing the unknowable is well-recorded in human history. It should never be underestimated, even in these so-called postmodern times. If our home is the place of refuge, comfort, and security for the body, then our faith is our source of refuge, comfort, and security for the soul.

If we lose our faith, perhaps then we lose our soul. Or perhaps we simply deny the soul as existing or having any relevance to our own existence. I don't know. What I do know from history, including our own history as Americans, is that a great many of us place a high level of importance to our faith. We are actively engaged in protecting our ability to practice our faith both in worship and the living of our daily lives. We resent the encroachment of our governmental alliances, particularly the Central Authority, on our practice of our faith at home and in our communities. Much of the current litigation over the national health-care law is motivated by faith.

In all the nations of America, we are a people of the God of Abraham. He is our Creator. We acknowledged

His presence in all that we did together to form our society here. We are people of the Bible, Jews and Christians. Our understanding of life and our understanding of our humanity, our frailty (sinfulness), our good decisions and bad decisions, and our relationship to our God all derive from the Holy Bible.

In communities throughout our land and in large swaths of the land itself, the Bible matters more than anyone can calculate. In other communities, principally our large urban centers, the Bible seems to matter less. Citizens who might fill out a survey as believers, are unchurched. Other citizens worship other gods or are nonbelievers.

Studying the several nations of either Garreau or Woodard, the different religious denominations do affect and inform their compatibility as members of one nation. But the differences do not seem to impact adversely our willingness to abide for necessity and convenience as an affiliated federal entity. Indeed, the commonality of faith in the Word of the Bible most likely enhanced the prospects for a compatible federal alliance.

However, as we experience the growing incompatibility of the Central Authority with our home and compatible communities, the differences in adherence to faith and its priority in our lives may become politically significant. Looking at the political maps in chapter 2, the Bible matters most in the red geography and least in the blue, according to available statistics of who is churched and where certain issues related to faith are paramount.[70] For example, most of the activity in state legislatures regarding the limitation of abortion and homosexual marriage are occurring in the red states.

The larger issue at work here is the matter of authority. For people of faith in the Word as given to us by God in the Bible, all authority rests with God, who, for Christians, gave the world His only son to teach us and save our souls for all eternity. We did not create God, as the nonbelievers assert. God created us. Life is a gift from God. We are His. The rite of Christian baptism makes each of us a "child of the covenant."

We can never be separated from His love or His authority.

We form governments of necessity and convenience to provide common services and order in our living. We grant to government its authority, the strength of which pales before the authority of God. Any allegiance we have to our government is that of an alliance of necessity and convenience, whereas our allegiance to God is one of adoration, worship, and awe. Government has no power over us. Only God has power over us.

In the first five books of the Bible, known as the Torah, God chooses Abraham to be the father of His people, who became known as the Israelites coming out of Egypt and delivered to the land promised by God. Along the way, God gave their leader, Moses, the Law to guide their living. The law is not just the Ten Commandments. The law as given to Moses and recorded by him in Deuteronomy is quite detailed.

God did not give His people a king. God advised strongly against kings. He told Moses that His people would want a king like all other nations, but that they must be very careful in their selection of their king.[71]

Initially, instead of kings, God gave the Israelites judges to facilitate organized society. Later God warned Samuel of the behavior of kings the people were demanding of Samuel to provide.[72] Earthly rulers are nothing but trouble as they subvert the will of the people to their own will.

The Israelites behaved in due time much like humans the world over have behaved then and now. They worshiped other gods. They wanted the security of kings to rule over them. And they ignored much, and sometimes all, of God's law. We know from the stories of the Israelites in the Old Testament that for over seven hundred years, things did not go well for them. They were conquered by others, split up, and relegated as a people to Judah, coming to be known in our language as Jews.

Then God brought the light into the world in the form of the prophet, Jesus of Nazareth, who Christians know as the Christ, the Messiah, the Son of God on earth. He preached a way of life that "render[s] unto Caesar what is Caesar's and unto God what is God's." Both Christians and Jews have had trouble understanding and living with this admonition for the past two thousand years. God warned both Moses and Samuel about kings. Men are weak and given to evil. Powerful men are given to more evil. How do we live God's law and abide evil rulers?

After 1,200 years of working at this problem, western mankind came up with the notions expressed in the Magna Carta and, five hundred years later, formed a constitutional republic in the American colonies. Perhaps a way was found to implement God's law and limit the corruption and evil of ruling power. We've been trying to work out this experiment for the past 238 years since our Declaration of Independence.

For those who don't know the Bible and adhere to its authority, we are simply making it all up as we go along. But for people of the Bible, we are trying to figure out how to adhere to God's law as community. The difference between the two notions is vast. We are speaking here of the arrogance of man versus the authority of God. We are speaking here of people who understand the importance and relevance of the history of the Jews as recorded in the Bible and of people who find much if not most history, including this history, to be irrelevant or recorded inaccurately and in need of revision.

Social arguments during our entire history have been defined more or less by teachings to us in the Bible versus popular will to the contrary. Those differences, including the current ones about gay marriage and abortion, pale to utter insignificance in the face of the present, growing, and suffocating monster of Central Authority ruling all. For those who believe in the Word of God as presented in the Bible, we are beset by a powerful force, possibly a form of evil, that cannot seem to be contained.

Christians are once again presented with the dilemma . . . do we render under Caesar what he will take from us, or do we resist? For the most part we abide. But in the end, we know that God's law will rule and that the people of faith in the teachings of the Bible will act. Our faith sustains us and, in the time of testing, will strengthen us.

The Day Cometh

Preparations

The American people who favor a Way of Life living under strictly limited authority, provision, and protection know that they are in the minority. They know that each election cycle has little meaning as their freedoms lessen. They know that our debt will crush us if we don't act to prevent it. The Tea Party Patriot movement (the 10 percenters) will grow in intensity and breadth of participation, providing the human energy necessary to effect interruptive change. They don't know what will happen, but they are getting prepared. They know that freedom will have a cost. When the day comes, they will be ready.

Inertia

In physics, inertia is a property of matter by which it continues in its existing state of rest or uniform motion in a straight line, unless changed by an external force. It is a tendency to do nothing or remain unchanged. This property or tendency can be of enormous strength, a great unmovable object.[73]

So it is with our American society at its current state of maturity. For regional leaders away from the Central Authority in business, law, medicine, and banking, life is good and comfortable, notwithstanding the frustration, anger, and growing alarm for our future. Many choose to devote their energies to local and regional philanthropic projects, shying away from confronting what lies ahead. Some choose to invest huge sums to effect political change on the national level. We do not choose confrontation and destabilizing change. There is too much to lose.

Our inertia is the avoidance of risk of loss from disruptive change. Our inertia is rational, sober, wise, and the mark of maturity. We understand the future may involve creation of two or more nation states from our current compliment of fifty states. This may happen, but it is not what we think about every day or do every day in our work and in our roles as leaders. Let's just go along and see what happens, influence what we can, and prosper as we can.

If we think about the regional leaders in the Way of Life land that advocates freedom of the individual and a government that protects but does not provide, we look in the western prairie to those in Dallas, Austin, Houston, San Antonio, Oklahoma City, Tulsa, Wichita, Kansas City, and Omaha. And if we examine the region we know as Dixie, the Deep South, we must look to Atlanta, Little Rock, New Orleans, Jackson, Birmingham, Montgomery, Charleston, and Greenville. In Appalachia, we would want to know about the leaders in Memphis, Nashville, Chattanooga, Knoxville, Lexington, Louisville, Wheeling, Parkersburg, and Charleston. Anywhere we look, we see the same sober resolve to work within the system, bide our time, wait, and see while doing what we can.

It is both unrealistic and perhaps unfair to assume or expect that the leaders in these regions will effect change on their own initiative unless they feel threatened personally in their profession, their property, or the security of their families. They are part of the 80 percent who rise every morning to go about their daily lives in peace. The impetus for interruptive change will be pressed upon them by others in their region in the 80 percent who they respect and whose needs they will honor and whose plight they will rally to rectify. Change will come from the working middle in their homes, their farms, and their factories who, for one reason or another, have been abused to an intolerable extent by the Central Authority. These affected citizens will move the leaders to act. Change will likely come from the bottom up, not top down.

The Pathway

The practical pathway to separation is likely to be secession by several states. State governments may be accidents of history as Garreau and Woodard have observed, but they already exist in functional form and provide an orderly means for peoples of a region to form their own more desirable (perfect) union. The nucleus of states to take the initial act will likely be all of one nation, sharing a common complaint, a common goal, and a common Way of Life. Other local, regional, and state governments who share this common Way of Life may then wish to separate themselves from their existing alliances of convenience and necessity to join this new nation.

Secession is not a new or radical subject. Quebec has been considering it for so long that it is no longer news. Catalonia in Spain will decide this autumn. Scotland is due for a vote this year as well. The north of England, including Yorkshire and the West Midlands, are not far behind.

In America, after the 2012 election, citizens from all states petitioned for the right to secede, and those from seven states exceeded the twenty-five thousand signature level to warrant an official response. Those states were Alabama, Florida, Georgia, Louisiana, North Carolina, Tennessee, and Texas, with the latter over 117,000 signatories. One mainstream publication that reported on these matters viewed such activities as of no significance, noting that secession is illegal and that most of these states receive more largess from the Central Authority than they pay.[74] And of course there is social security, national defense, and the currency.

Secession is messy, to be sure, but need not be all that difficult in our current society, especially if the seceding group is significant. The majority of Americans voting for Central Authority power are doing so to preserve the income support of a welfare state. It is only the 10 percenters, or an even smaller minority, that are bent on controlling everyone and bringing them into human bondage to their Way of Life. The

80 percent blue state citizens want their subsidies, checks, and grants from the Central Authority. They do not want to fight anyone nor do they want to control anyone. There is no fight to be had here.

The federal government is bankrupt, so there are no spoils to be had. There is only the debt to apportion. Any new union of states will have to figure out how they intend to govern themselves and manage their future together.

Certainly the small minority enjoying the power of the Central Authority is likely to be vicious in its response to even the threat of secession. We have seen its reaction to the Sequester at the end of 2012, warning the American people of dire consequences and threatening actions to make Americans suffer for failing to force the Congress to behave as the Central Authority demanded. We have seen its reaction to the threat of organized and well-funded political speech opposed to Central Authority power when it co-opted the Internal Revenue Service to harass and threaten these citizen groups.

The Central Authority is certainly capable of violence, and some may occur. Yet nothing in our national behavior of the past half century would suggest the support of violence by citizens of the blue states who otherwise accept a Way of Life protected and provided by a Central Authority. If I am wrong in this judgment, we are headed for a second civil war. But I just don't see this in our future.

Catalysts

Any attempt to identify the catalyst is strictly a guessing game of pure speculation. It may be one of the following discussed here or something altogether different and unexpected.

A Last Election

Since we are worn to exasperation over our divisiveness and its adverse consequences in our daily lives, we could expect an election to occur that is deemed decisive. Suppose that after the 2014, 2016, or 2018 election a large swath of America clustered in the so-called red states were to realize that it is permanently disenfranchised, much the same as the South realized as 1860 elections approached after the free state/ slave state balance was broken. The Tea Party Patriots and other politically energized groups within these states could pressure governors and key legislators to caucus with other similarly disenfranchised leaders in neighboring states. This activity might develop a momentum of its own that becomes unstoppable. The 10 percenters would move the 80 percent.

A Thief in the Night

Like Ferguson's thief in the night, America's dollar ceases to be the world's reserve currency as our military is unable or unwilling to defend America's interests (and others) across the globe. Interest rates on our debt rise dramatically, the Central Authority prints dollars, hyperinflation occurs, and all is lost for half the country, most of whom live off the government in urban environments. What follows is the breakdown in urban public order with riots, looting, and lawlessness. America becomes Argentina.

The Argentina outcome is arguably quite likely in due course at our current pace. United States influence on the world stage is declining at an alarming rate. Our economy remains in first gear or on idle. Our Federal Reserve continues to print money.

The ensuing collapse would consume the resources of the Homeland Security officers who have been delivering crowd-control SWAT-tank-type vehicles to urban police departments in preparation for widespread urban violence. Such a breakdown in the civil order would provide a convenient opportunity for regional nations to secede and form their own independent nation states. The entire continent would be in for a very rough patch, and our friends abroad would be abused and exploited with no support from America. Not a pretty vision. But it could happen.

Central Authority Last Straw

More likely as the catalyst, I envision, will be an incursion by the Central Authority into one of our homes that is judged utterly intolerable by the home population. We are well past the tipping point of Central Authority incursions. It seems, then, simply a matter of time when an incursion will occur that is the veritable straw to break the back.

The last straw is likely not to be in the realm of incursion upon our ability to exercise our faith. With respect to these abuses, the home population expresses its own form of lamentation, not wholly dissimilar from Friedman and Mandelbaum, but truly mournful. This mournfulness will not, of itself, be likely to cause violence or even secession but will indeed grease the wheels of justification when the time comes. People of faith will endure untold abuse and abide. They will also countenance and succor their fellow like-minded community members who elect to resist an intolerable physical incursion into their homes, farms, or factories. Faith is the support for action, not the catalyst.

The last straw could well be an intrusion in the home so abusive and violent as to cause the citizens of the home community to rise up in fear, anger, and resolve. The entering of homes to seize firearms on a broad scale, perhaps, could drive such a reaction. The Central Authority is quite capable of this behavior, particularly under the color of some fabricated ruse, citing a threat to public safety. We would like to think that we learned a lesson from the tragedy near Waco, Texas, during the Clinton administration, but our history lessons are weak these days. A physical incursion is certainly possible but hopefully will not occur.

It could be an action by the Central Authority which effectively disenfranchises the citizens of a region. The Central Authority is attempting to succeed in this game in Texas and the Carolinas by ignoring the Supreme Court's judgment in the area of state voter registration laws and suing the states to bend their will to the

Central Authority view. Such activity could rise to the level that invites separation.

More likely, it seems, is an incursion into our work at home or on our farms or in our factories that stifles our ability to earn a livelihood. New rules to restrain and restrict commerce are routine activities of the Central Authority. The incursion that proves to be the last straw will be considered routine, necessary, and desirable by the Central Authority bureaucrats either to teach a lesson (as the Oklahoma EPA administrator instructed a few years ago and that OSHA did to the Nebraska farm family) or to exercise their perceived mandate and ingratiate themselves to the special interest groups from which they were appointed to their role as regulator and rule maker. The incursion will be large enough geographically to include citizens in more than one state, and it will be significant enough to materially harm the economies of the affected regions. The incursion will likely seem rather benign and perhaps silly to society at large not directly affected in their home, farm, or factory.

These incursions by the Central Authority are occurring regularly. I don't know which one will be the spark that ignites the brush fire that blows out of control across our land. How about chickens? Maybe even a certain chicken of a lesser type. Have you ever heard of the lesser prairie chicken? It is a type of grouse that roams the southwestern prairie lands of five states including parts of Kansas, Oklahoma, Texas, Colorado, and New Mexico. It fears tall structures like barns, wind turbines, oil rigs, power lines, and even fences where its predator, the hawk, can perch and spot it. And its population is declining lately, in no small measure due to the drought in the region.

Environmental and animal rights groups based in the wilderness regions of Washington, DC, and San Francisco sued the Fish and Wildlife Service, a unit of the Central Authority Department of the Interior, to declare the species threatened or endangered under the Endangered Species Act. The Fish and Wildlife Service settled the lawsuit by agreeing to place the bird on the threatened species list, which it announced March 27, 2014. Oklahoma filed suit against Fish and Wildlife, challenging the sue-and-settle ruse used by the greenies and their Central Authority fellow travelers to bypass the rule-making process required under federal law.[75]

This incursion in the five-state region is not really about the bird. The wildlife agencies in these states have been working for many years (and millions of dollars) over a three-million-acre area to try to preserve this bird. This incursion is about fossil fuels, oil, and gas. It is about restricting development of the huge Permian Basin in Texas and New Mexico on private land.

It is about stopping the Keystone pipeline to bring fuel from Canada. It is about Central Authority control directed by very wealthy urban-living environmentalists who are committed to forcing the American people to live on this earth their way.

There is no right or wrong here. There is no great human moral. There is only the matter of who will judge the work behavior in this regional homeland— the people at home or the people in Central Authority in Washington, DC. Maybe it will be a lesser prairie chicken that sets a fire. Maybe it will be the rabbitsfoot mussel, Sprague's pipit, or the Arkansas darter. All are in the endangered species pipeline. Or maybe it will be one of the seven-hundred-plus other species forced on to the list by two recent sue-and-settle cases against Fish and Wildlife.

The beleaguered and angry people of the region who are losing their jobs, losing the value of their land, losing their communities, losing their freedom to live their traditional life in their homeland will reach out to their legislatures for action. The only rational reaction, after lawsuits turn out to be futile, might be the realization that separation must be brought to occur.

In the example above, the catalyst would be an incursion in the homeland region by the Central Authority that denies these citizens the ability to continue to earn their traditional livelihood in their homes, farms, and factories. Texas might use the tactic of terminating their treaty relationship with the United States, and Oklahoma might then secede to join a union with Texas. Kansas might follow shortly. There is little federal land in either Oklahoma, Kansas, or Texas to fight over. These three states are a large region with a robust and diverse economy, able to govern themselves, produce an independent livelihood, have access to the sea, and function independently.

The Deep South would be attracted to this new alliance. Dixie is no friend of the Central Authority and might well opt for a new pathway. A reasonable speculation would see South Carolina, Alabama, Mississippi, Louisiana, and Arkansas joining a union with Texas within months. Georgia would join reluctantly, perhaps first trying to claim the capital for Atlanta, but finally acknowledging that they need to be allied with their neighbors. At the same time, Appalachia would likely move as well. Tennessee and Kentucky would join Texas to preserve their coal industry. Florida would find itself isolated and would also join after being assured by the new union that retirement security benefits could be maintained. One could speculate further that North Carolina and Missouri would take the leap. When the flurry of activity during a nine-month period is over, the map of America might look like the following:

| United States of America | 36 States | (white) |
| New American States | 14 States | (lined) |

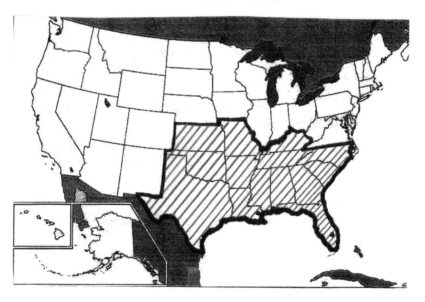

The fourteen states on the map above would comprise a formidable independent nation state. The manner in which this alliance chose to determine its governance would be observed by all the remaining thirty-six states.

The map above leaves open the many next phases of decision making by Americans observing these developments. Which way would Virginia lean, and what of the great naval port at Norfolk? Would Virginia break down by counties, some allying with the South and some the North? What would happen in West Virginia and in the southern counties of Ohio, Indiana, and Illinois?

In the northern plains to the Continental Divide, the culture is not friendly to the Central Authority. Would Montana, Wyoming, the Dakotas, and Nebraska form their own union perhaps with Colorado, Utah, and Idaho, or might they wish to join the Texas alliance, or remain with the old union? In the far west, Garreau's Ecotopia and Woodard's Left Coast do not embrace the central valleys of California agriculture or the empty lands east of the Cascades to the north. Would the people in these lands ally themselves with their neighbors to the east? And what of Arizona, New Mexico, and Alaska?

For certain, there would be a great awakening and much debate throughout the land if Texas, Oklahoma, and Kansas, as an example, were to secede and form a new alliance. In the end, there would be two or more new American nation states forming a puzzle yet to be etched in history.

It should not matter to us as people on this continent how our fellow citizens decide to form themselves compatibly. Separating ourselves into more compatible nations of similar cultural mores would remove the distraction and huge cost of divisiveness, permitting us to reset our institutions to our needs as we perceive them in our separate culture. Congress has the constitutional power under Article IV, Section 3 to admit new states to the Union. Nowhere does the Constitution prevent the Congress from permitting states to exit the Union and form new alliances.

In fact, the most peaceful pathway to human freedom and the end of destructive divisiveness on this continent would be for the United States Congress to pass a law permitting states to separate themselves from the United States by vote of their legislative bodies and for counties to be able to separate themselves from States to join other states or alliances. Doing so would create the possibility for more compatible societies. Human freedom would prevail throughout the land.

My Vision

What I see in our future is a robust reawakening of both desire and ability in our several nations in North America to form our own destinies, to live in this land as free men and women, to reform ourselves in creating a Way of Life suitable to our homes, farms, and factories where we live and suitable to our faith.

I see a North American continent alive again with creative work, wealth generation, and growth unorchestrated and exciting.

I see people of our many nations living the life God gave us in many different ways, celebrating our human freedom and joining together for our common defense.

I see boundless choices for the children and grandchildren of this continent as they grow to maturity learning of the vitality and energy unleashed across the land.

I see a richness of life worth living and therefore worth dying to preserve for those who follow.

I see a renewed America of several American nations that as a whole deserve my loyalty and my love.

I see this renewed America as once again the light of the world.

May God bless America.

Notes

Chapter One: Killing the Empire

1. Fictitious cover boy of *Mad Magazine*. See Alfred E. Neuman, *Wikipedia*.
2. Niall Ferguson, *Civilization* (Penguin Group, 2011), 299.
3. Ibid., 292.
4. Ibid., 302-303.
5. Ibid., 303.
6. Ibid., 12-13.
7. Tariff Act of 1930, *Wikipedia*.
8. "Tally of US Banks Sinks to Record Low," WSJ.com, Dec. 3, 2013.
9. Nuclear Power in the United States, *Wikipedia*.
10. National Archives Public Website. Also Code of Federal Regulations, *Wikipedia*.
11. ABA Market Research Department, American Bar Association (2012).
12. Ferguson, *Civilization*, 262.
13. Charles Murray, *Coming Apart* (Random House, 2012), 173.
14. Ibid., 188.
15. US Census Bureau Published Data.

16. Ibid. Also *Wall Street Journal,* March 28, 2013, A1 and A12 and July 13, 2013, A12.
17. Murray, *Coming Apart,* 169.
18. Ibid., 170-171.
19. Michael Tanner and Charles Hughes, *The Work Versus Welfare Trade-Off: 2013* (Cato Institute, 2013).
20. Office of Management and Budget, US Government, Historical Tables.
21. In the author's food processing business with a low value added to labor ratio relative to most US manufacturing industries, the ration of sales value to direct labor cost at the margin is 10:1.
22. Pogo (comic strip), *Wikipedia.*
23. Ferguson, *Civilization,* 323.

Chapter Two: Divided We Stand

24. Peter Schiff, *Wall Street Journal,* December 7, 2012, A17.
25. Murray, *Coming Apart,* 223-225.
26. Ibid., 276-277.
27. Ibid., 285-294.

Sources of Reference:

Bureau of Labor Statistics, "Union Members Summary," news release, January 23, 2013.

Internal Revenue Service Historical Tax Tables and Income Spreads.

Joint Economic Committee, Republican Staff Commentary, "The Pending State Pensions Crisis," September 26, 2012.

Morgan, John, "Unfunded Federal Pension Liabilities Head
    Skyward" (February 22, 2013), Money News.Com.
Pew Charitable Trusts, "A Widening Gap in Cities," January
    2013.
Tax Policy Center, Urban Institute and Brookings
    Institution, Individual Income Tax Data.
US Office of Personnel Management, "Historical Federal
    Workforce Tables," July 24, 2013.

Chapter Three: Two Ways of Life

28. Fergus M. Bordewich, *America's Great Debate* (Simon &
    Schuster, 2012).
29. Ibid., 126.
30. Ibid., 81.
31. Ibid., 114-122.
32. Ibid., 121.
33. Ibid., 135-137 (the author lists eight resolutions offered
    by Clay).
34. Ibid., 329.
35. Scott v. Sandford, 60 US 393.
36. Ibid., 10.
37. Ibid., 11.
38. Nicolay and Hay, "Mr. Lincoln's Reply in the Alton
    Joint Debate, October 15, 1858," *The Complete Works of
    Abraham Lincoln*, v. 5, Tandy Company, 1894, published
    by permission, Northern Illinois University Digitization
    Projects, para. 65.
39. Gautham Nagesh, *Wall Street Journal*, February 14, 2014.
40. Erskine Bowles and Alan Simpson, "The Moment of
    Truth," National Commission on Fiscal Responsibility
    and Reform, December 1, 2010.

41. Jackie Calmes, "'Gang of Six' in the Senate Seeking a Plan on Debt," *The New York Times*, April 16, 2011.

42. National Federation of Independent Business, et. al. v. Sibelius, Secretary of Health and Human Services, et.al., No. 11-393, June 28, 2012, 567 U.S.____(2012).

43. Lobbying Data Base, Open Secrets.org.

44. Tarini Parti, *Politico*, January 31, 2013.

45. Kristine A. Tidgren, "Senators Challenge OSHA's Attempts to Regulate Small Farm Grain Bins," Iowa State University, Center for Agricultural Law and Taxation, January 9, 2014.

Chapter Four: Fraying the Common Thread

46. Alexis de Tocqueville, *Democracy in America*, vol. 2, book 1 (Schocken Books, 1961), 2.

47. Ibid.

48. Colin Woodard, *American Nations* (Penguin Books, 2011).

49. Ibid., 3.

50. Ibid.

51. Arthur M. Schlesinger, Jr., *The Disuniting of America* (W.W. Norton & Company, 1992).

52. Ibid., 123.

53. Ibid., 17.

54. Ibid., 137.

55. Ibid., 133.

56. Thomas Friedman and Michael Mandelbaum, *That Used To Be Us* (Picador/Farrar, Straus and Geroux, 2011).

57. Ibid., 18-19.

58. Ibid., 22.

59. Ibid., 36.

60. Ibid., 37.

61. Ibid., 304.
62. Kovacs, Holman, and Jackson, "Sue and Settle" (US Chamber of Commerce, 2013).

Chapter Five: The Essence of Life

63. Joel Garreau, *The Nine Nations of North America* (Houghton Mifflin Company, 1981).
64. Ibid., 159.
65. Ibid., 1.
66. Ibid., xiv.
68. Ibid., xvi.
68. Ibid., 13.
69. Ibid., 137.
70. Frank Newport, "State of the States," March 27, 2012 and February 17, 2010 (Gallup, Inc., 2014).
71. Deuteronomy 17:14, Holy Bible, (New International Version) International Bible Society, 1973, 1978, 1984.
72. 1 Samuel 8:1-8.

Chapter Six: The Day Cometh

73. *Concise Oxford English Dictionary* (Oxford University Press, 2011).
74. *The Economist*, December 1, 2012, 34
75. Jay F. Marks, "Oklahoma Attorney General, energy group, sue US Fish and Wildlife Service over endangered species settlements," *Fox News First Newsletter* (March 17, 2014).

Index